hamlyn | all colour petcare

puppy taming

The easy route to a happy, obedient dog

Edited by Caroline Davis

hamlyn

An Hachette UK Company
www.hachette.co.uk

First published in Great Britain in 2009 by
Hamlyn, a division of Octopus Publishing Group Ltd
2–4 Heron Quays, London E14 4JP
www.octopusbooks.co.uk

ISBN 978-0-600-61826-3

A CIP catalogue record for this book is
available from the British Library

Printed and bound in China

10 9 8 7 6 5 4 3 2 1

Note Unless the information is specific to males or
females, throughout this book puppies and dogs are
referred to as 'he' and the information and advice are
applicable to both sexes.

The advice in this book is provided as general
information only. It is not necessarily specific to
any individual case and is not a substitute for
the guidance and advice provided by a licensed
veterinary practitioner consulted in any particular
situation. Octopus Publishing Group accepts no
liability or responsibility for any consequences
resulting from the use of or reliance upon the
information contained herein. No puppies were
harmed in the making of this book.

Contents

Perfect pals **6**

First impressions **32**

At your bidding **58**

Puppy meets the world **90**

Understanding your puppy **104**

Etiquette in the home **132**

Out and about **164**

My puppy's a genius! **178**

Index **188**

Acknowledgements **192**

Perfect pals

Choosing a puppy

Fantastic! You've decided to get a puppy and choosing one to share your life is exciting. You'll be keen to pick your perfect doggy pal, but first take a little time to think about which will be the best type of puppy for you.

Living together

To ensure you get the dog of your dreams, and he in turn thinks you are the best owner ever, you need to consider breed, size and type. It's important that a puppy fits comfortably into your lifestyle so that potential problems are minimized. There are three types of puppy to choose from.

Pure-bred (pedigree) These can be expensive to buy. Read up about the many different breeds, so that for each one you know what to expect in terms of size, temperament and character, as well as the ailments from which some breeds tend to suffer. For example, a Dobermann needs lots of room and exercise while a tiny Chihuahua requires neither. A Cavalier King Charles Spaniel is generally thought of as an excellent all-round family pet.

Cross-bred Not as expensive as pedigrees to buy, a cross-bred puppy has pedigree parents of different breeds. Knowing what the parents are like, you have a fair idea of what to expect in terms of appearance and character. Generally, breeders will cross two particular breeds to get the best characteristics of both, or perhaps a catchy

name. For example, the Labradoodle is a cross between a Labrador and a Poodle, while a CockerPoo is a Cocker Spaniel crossed with a Poodle!

Mongrel Inexpensive to buy or even free, a mongrel puppy results when one or both parents are cross-breds or mongrels themselves. With his lineage generally unknown, this pup's appearance, size and character may turn out to be something of a surprise! Mongrels are generally more robust than some of their pedigree counterparts and range from small to large, smooth- to long-coated, and come in a wonderful array of shapes and colours.

Happy times ahead

Whatever type you go for, whether it be a sleek and haughty Saluki or a happy and scruffy mongrel, as long as you ensure you are the owner every dog would want you should be able to look forward to a long and happy partnership.

Consider your lifestyle

Once you have decided on pure-bred, cross-bred or mongrel, the next step is to check out which types tick all the right boxes for you in terms of companionship and lifestyle. Aim to pick the perfect partner – then it's less likely to end in tears!

Puppy profile

Take into account the following:

- Are you energetic and do you want a dog that will enjoy long walks and other sporty activities?
- Do you have children who hanker after having a pet?
- If you don't have much house space, do you simply want a dog as a lovable companion and friend?

- Or do you have plenty of space, inside and out, and would adore a doggy friend to share it with you?

Busy bees If you are an energetic person who wants to enjoy more strenuous activities and walks with your pet, go for a type that can cope with plenty of physical exertion. Lively types like the Border Collie need plenty of daily exercise, while some dogs are bred specifically for sporting activities, such as flushing out and retrieving game, like the Irish Water Spaniel.

Gentle pals A friendly, easy-going type of dog is ideal for a less energetic person and for children. For the former, a Greyhound is ideal – despite his speedy looks and ability, he is the archetypal couch potato who adores snuggling up and lazing the day away with his owner.

Loving companions Some dogs are more affectionate than others, so if you want a really lovable pet read up on the various breeds to help you pick a puppy that adores cuddles, such as a Shih Tzu.

Hairy hounds Some breeds, such as the Golden Retriever, need grooming on a regular basis; others, such as the Poodle, need attention from a canine beautician about every six weeks. If you don't feel you can cope with the time, effort and expense involved in canine hairdressing, it's a good idea to pick a puppy with a low-maintenance coat type such as a Border Terrier or – going to the extreme – a Mexican Hairless!

Still not sure which breed is best for you? Turn to pages 12–13 for lifestyle examples and the breeds that might suit them.

Choosing a puppy

No two people, or puppies, are ever the same, but the five at-a-glance guides provided in the charts on these pages will show you which breeds are suited to different situations and may help you decide on your final choice of four-legged friend.

YOUNG, ACTIVE COUPLE

Large house; remote rural area; lots of off-lead exercise opportunities

Experienced owners; require security/watchdog and companionship

MEDIUM TO GIANT DOG PREFERRED

Hair and slobber OK	Prefer easy-care coat
Afghan Hound	Bloodhound
Borzoi	Bullmastiff
Briard	Dobermann
Leonberger	English Springer Spaniel
Longhaired German Shepherd	Great Dane
Newfoundland	Irish Wolfhound
Rough Collie	Lurcher
Scottish Deerhound	Pointers
St Bernard	Rhodesian Ridgeback
	Rottweiler
	Setters
	Shorthaired German Shepherd

ACTIVE PERSON

Small house and garden; built-up residential area; off-lead exercise requires car journey

Experienced owner; requires active, happy pet for exercise and companionship

SMALL DOG PREFERRED

Requires easy-care smooth coat	No objection to grooming
Boston Terrier	Affenpinscher
Chihuahua	American/English Cocker Spaniel
Jack Russell Terrier	Bedlington Terrier
Lancashire Heeler	Border Terrier
Smooth-haired Dachshund	Cavalier/King Charles Spaniel
Whippet	Dandie Dinmont Terrier
	Maltese
	Miniature/Toy Poodle
	Pomeranian
	West Highland White Terrier
	Yorkshire Terrier

SENIOR COUPLE

Limited mobility; small house and garden

Experienced owners; require security/watchdog and companionship

---

ANY SIZE OK, ALTHOUGH SMALL DOG PREFERRED

Prefer easy-care coat	High-maintenance coat OK
Chihuahua	Bichon Frise
Chinese Crested	Cavalier/King Charles
Corgi	Spaniel
Dandie Dinmont Terrier	Lhasa Apso
Greyhound	Longhaired Dachshund
Italian Greyhound	Maltese
Pug	Miniature/Toy Poodle
Schipperke	Pekinese
	Shih Tzu

FAMILY WITH YOUNG CHILDREN

Large detached house and garden; residential area

First-time owners; require friendly, fun family companion and watchdog

---

MEDIUM TO LARGE DOG PREFERRED

Prefer easy-care coat	Medium-maintenance coat OK
Beagle	
Boston Terrier	Bearded Collie
Greyhound	Bernese Mountain Dog
Labrador Retriever	Golden Retriever
Schipperke	Newfoundland
Smooth Collie	Rough Collie
Whippet	Shetland Sheepdog

MIDDLE-AGED COUPLE

Average-sized semi-detached house and large garden; rural area; enjoy walking and home travel

Experienced owners; require kind, fun, active dog for companionship and outings

---

MEDIUM TO LARGE DOG PREFERRED

Medium-maintenance coat OK	Prefer easy-care coat
Airedale Terrier	Basenji
Border Collie	Boxer
English Cocker/	Dalmatian
Springer Spaniel	Dobermann
Golden Retriever	Greyhound
Rough Collie	Hungarian Vizsla
Schnauzers	Labrador Retriever
Setters	Pharaoh Hound
Siberian Husky	Pointers
Standard Poodle	Rhodesian Ridgeback
	Rottweiler
	Shorthaired German Shepherd
	Smooth Collie
	Weimaraner

Puppy shopping

You've decided which breed of puppy will suit you – now all you have to do is find him! There are several options as to where to get your friend, all of which have advantages and disadvantages, so the choice is yours once you have assessed them.

Finding your puppy

Breeders' advertisements, pet stores, vets' noticeboards, dog magazines, animal shelters, and friends and family are all potential sources. You may even find a stray.

A puppy should be at least six weeks old before he leaves his mother and fully weaned onto puppy food. Ideally, he should have been socialized with a wide range of people and other animals. Some breeders prefer to wait until their puppies are a little older, fully toilet trained and have had their initial vaccinations.

Dog breeder Select a puppy from a whole litter if possible. Pick one that seems healthy (see pages 120–121), outgoing, frisky and friendly, and approaches you confidently.

Friends and family With a puppy acquired in this way, you have a good chance of knowing who the parents are and how he will turn out.

vets' waiting rooms, and getting the puppy checked by your vet for a microchip.

Pet store or 'puppy farm' (multi-breed kennel). Unfortunately, if many pups are kept together in a less-than-ideal environment and there is a constant turnover of 'stock', there is an ever-present risk of infection. Buying your puppy from such places is not to be recommended.

How much is that puppy in the window?

The price of a puppy depends on his type and where you get him from.

Dog breeder Depends on the breed and whether or not the puppy is show quality. It pays to shop around.

Friends and family Varies from free to very expensive!

Animal shelter There is usually a charge to cover neutering and vaccinations.

Stray Free.

Pet store or puppy farm Depends on the breed or type.

Animal shelter Find out as much as you can from the staff about your chosen puppy's background, but you will have to bear in mind that a pup from such a place is often an unknown quantity.

Stray Occasionally, you may come across an 'abandoned' puppy – however, he may simply be lost. Try to trace his owners by informing local animal welfare shelters, putting up 'found' posters in local stores and

Puppy paraphernalia

For many people, one of the most enjoyable things about getting a puppy is going shopping. There is a massive selection of beds and bowls, toys and treats, leads and lots of other great gear guaranteed to make a hole in your pocket!

Puppy must-haves

There are some essential items you will need to buy for your new puppy before he arrives home. All these are available from pet stores, supermarkets or via the internet – your budget will dictate how much you spend and also the quality of the items you buy, which can vary considerably. Alternatively, you could try having a puppy shower. Invite friends and family for a get-together, but on the proviso that they must bring your puppy a present; you could even circulate a list!

Identity disc With your name and telephone number.

Food and water bowls Buy heavy bowls that your puppy can't tip over. They should be easy to clean and non-chewable: you don't want him getting a blockage or excreting plastic! Water bowls should be large enough to contain a day's supply.

Bed You can use an indoor crate, or buy a bed big enough to accommodate your puppy when he's mature.

Bedding Buy new from a pet store or use old blankets. Old towels are useful for drying off a wet dog.

Toys A chewy toy, a ball and toys that dispense treats when played with will all get the thumbs-up from your pup!

Grooming kit You'll need a comb, brush and dog shampoo. Brushing your puppy's teeth with a toothbrush and dog toothpaste will help to keep his teeth free from plaque build-up and periodontal disease.

Collar and lead Choose a 'kind' collar, such as a broad collar in leather or synthetic

material, of the appropriate weight and width for your puppy's size. These are often considered more suitable than a half-check collar, the efficacy of which is often debated.

Poop scoop Alternatively, use old plastic carriers or food bags. Dispose of faeces in public dog wastebins or with your household rubbish (check with your local authority).

Useful extras

Indoor kennel or crate Handy in the home and car.

Dog guard For car travel safety.

Dog coat To keep thin-coated breeds warm in chilly weather.

Dinner's served!

The way to a puppy's heart is definitely through his stomach. Feed him a controlled and well-balanced diet, plus a few treats, and he'll love you forever – and be bounding with health, sporting a glossy coat and sparkling eyes.

Food and drink

Puppies grow quickly and need 2½ times more calories per unit of bodyweight than mature dogs. It's important to give your pup the right food in the correct amounts. His tummy is small, so divide his food into small feeds given several times a day.

Your puppy's breeder or vet should be happy to give you a diet sheet that covers what food to give, how much and when. Stick to this for as long as is recommended to avoid your new puppy suffering a digestive upset. He will also need a constant supply of fresh water.

Mastering menus

Proprietary brands of puppy food are easy to feed and contain all the nutrients your pet needs. Some large and giant breeds, like Great Danes, need special diets to ensure they don't grow too fast, so some types of puppy food may not be suitable – check with the vet. Generally, however, if you choose a 'famous name' brand containing minimal artificial ingredients (particularly colourings) you won't go far wrong.

Bones and treats

Count food treats as part of your puppy's calorie intake to ensure he doesn't become

obese. Again, it is best to choose those with as few artificial ingredients as possible, as these can cause behavioural and other health problems in some dogs.

It is a good idea to let your puppy gnaw on large, raw, meaty marrowbones or cooked, sterilized bones which you can buy from pet stores, since these help to keep his teeth and gums in tip-top condition. Dispose of them when they begin to go 'off' or break up. Be careful, though, never to give your puppy poultry or other small bones such as ribs and chops that may splinter.

Daily meals

Here's a guide to a puppy's daily feeding requirements:

- **Weaning to 20 weeks** Four meals, plus baby or puppy formula milk at night
- **20–30 weeks** Three meals
- **30 weeks to 9 months** Two meals (depending on breed and growth rate)
- **Over 9 months** One to two meals

Don't forget to wash food and water bowls daily. Dirty bowls are a health hazard and may put your puppy off eating and drinking.

Home comforts

To ensure that your home is a perfect puppy palace in which your new pal will be healthy and happy, you need to check it out thoroughly. This way, both he and your belongings will stay safe and sound.

Precious playthings

Your home may suit you well, but will it be a safe and comfortable haven for your puppy? If you tend to leave precious belongings lying around, you will now have to put them out of the way. Such items are fair game – and a possible health hazard – for an inquisitive puppy, who will play with and chew whatever he can get his teeth into. Until he is trained to leave things that aren't his alone, you can't expect him to do so.

Puddles and muddles

Emotions always run high when a puppy arrives, so you will have to tell yourself to remain calm – even in the face of adversity. Remember that your puppy will be feeling quite stressed for some time, so it's important to realize that things might not go as smoothly as you imagined. Try to stay relaxed if the unexpected happens, such as finding a puddle on your carpet. Keeping your sense of humour is vital!

Happy families

There are lots of positive things you can do to give your puppy's new life a happy start.

- Keep your pet in a 'puppy-proof' area of the house where he can do minimal damage – to himself as well – until he's settled down and is toilet trained.
- Remember that he's small and squirmy, and can get into and under things from which he can't escape.
- Move or secure electrical cables out of reach in case your puppy chews them.
- Close toilet lids to prevent an adventurous puppy climbing in!
- Always run cold water into the bath before hot in case your puppy gets in. Better still, keep bathroom doors closed at all times.
- Put notices on appliances such as the oven or washing machine urging everyone to check before closing the door. These can be inviting places for him to take a nap.
- Don't leave food or drinks on tables at puppy height: he will sample them!

Garden safety

A garden to play in, with its many exciting scents, nooks and crannies just waiting to be explored, is every dog's dream. Take steps to ensure it doesn't turn into a nightmare by carefully puppy-proofing your new pet's adventure playground.

Plug those gaps

If you are busy doing something and don't need your puppy's help, it's very handy to be able to let him out into the garden while you finish your task. It pays, however, to take a good look at your garden before you bring your new puppy home to make sure it will be completely safe for him.

Puppies are agile and capable of getting through the tiniest of gaps, so hunt around for any space that a canine Houdini might wriggle through and secure it well. If he manages to get out, he will be at risk of disease and attack from other dogs, a traffic accident or being stolen.

Scrapyard scrapes

A garden or yard that resembles a scrapyard is no place for a dog, so remove any rubbish,

implements and broken glass that could injure him. Time spent clearing up could well save you a fortune in vet's bills.

Beware if you use pellets and pesticides to get rid of garden pests. Those that are not pet-safe may get rid of your puppy, too, if he eats contaminated insects or helps himself to garden chemicals left accessible to him.

If you accidentally spill a chemical such as car anti-freeze or oil, clean it up immediately in case your puppy fancies a taste or paddles through it and then ingests it later when he licks himself.

Do put up a 'Puppy playing out – please close the gate' sign to alert visitors.

Plants and ponds

Many plants and shrubs can be poisonous to your puppy, so it's a good idea to research this and remove or fence off any dangers.

Ponds and swimming pools, however, seem to have a magnetic effect on an adventurous puppy, who is likely to drown if he falls in and cannot get out. If you cannot put a non-slip, gently sloping ramp in your water feature, either fence it off so your puppy can't get near it or don't allow him into the garden unattended. Buckets filled with rainwater can also prove fatal for a small pup, so store these and watertight tubs upside down when not in use.

Puppy pampering

Creating the ideal puppy haven of tranquillity, combined with periods of entertainment to feed his mind, exercise to keep him fit and good food to fill his belly, really pays dividends. Get it right and your puppy will be happy – and so will you!

Think dog

Sometimes it's tempting to pamper your puppy to the maximum, but as long as you consider his needs in relation to what he is – a dog – all will be well. Your puppy won't be any more contented with a diamond collar than a nylon one: what is important to him is that it fits properly and he can forget he's wearing it. Equally, the most expensive dog bed in the world will be uninviting if it's placed in a draught or next to a radiator that gets too hot.

It's little things like this you must consider to make sure your puppy feels your home is the best place he can be.

Reality check

Of course you can spoil your puppy, but make sure it's in the right way. For example, you might imagine he would love to share your curry, washed down with a swig of beer and followed by a helping of chocolate pudding. Being inherently greedy, most pups would scoff all this with relish – and ask for more. But this type of food is not good for him: in fact, chocolate can prove fatal to dogs, young or old. At the very least, such a spicy, boozy meal will cause flatulence, make your puppy feel ill and upset his stomach.

What your puppy will enjoy just as much, if not more because there are no unpleasant side effects, is five minutes of your time playing with him in the garden.

Room service please!

Puppies don't feel guilty, because they are unable to assimilate such a feeling. What they do display is fear, which many owners mistake for 'guilt'. Similarly, owners mistake pleading eyes at teatime for desperate hunger, when in fact all your puppy is doing is training you in the art of room service!

Attributing human emotions and requirements (known as anthropomorphism) to a puppy is to everyone's detriment. Treat your canine pal like the dog he is, for everyone's ultimate benefit.

Recipes for success

If you're a dab hand in the kitchen, why not have a go at rustling up some extra-special food treats for your puppy? Not only are these goodies easy to make, but you'll also know they're fresh and don't contain lots of colourings and other additives.

KENNEL KISS COOKIES

These healthy biscuits will help to keep your puppy's kisses sweet.

Makes 8–10 biscuits
Preparation time 15 minutes
Cooking time 40 minutes

125 g (4 oz) plain flour,
  plus extra for rolling
25 g (1 oz) cornmeal
2 tablespoons dried mint
3 tablespoons dried parsley
50 ml (2 fl oz) water
6 tablespoons vegetable oil
sunflower seeds

1 Preheat the oven to 180°C (350°F), Gas Mark 4. Grease a baking tray or use a nonstick one. Put all the ingredients except the sunflower seeds in a large bowl and mix thoroughly.

2 Roll out the dough to 5 mm (¼ inch) thick on a floured surface, then cut into shapes with biscuit cutters.

3 Decorate the shapes with sunflower seeds and place them on the baking tray. Bake until lightly browned.

4 Allow the biscuits to dry out in a warm place for several hours. Store in an airtight container to keep them crisp.

BARKER'S BIRTHDAY CAKE

Celebrate your puppy's birthday in style
by baking this cool canine confection!
Don't spoil him too much though – as
with humans, it's best to save sugary
treats for special occasions.

Serves 4–16
Preparation time 10 minutes
Cooking time 30 minutes

175 g (6 oz) self-raising
  wholemeal flour
50 g (2 oz) demerara sugar
2 tablespoons dried skimmed milk
2 small eggs, beaten
5 tablespoons cold water
2 generous tablespoons
  clear honey
4 generous tablespoons
  mascarpone cheese
dog chocolates and birthday
  candles and holders to decorate

1 Preheat the oven to 180°C (350°F), Gas Mark
4. Grease two 18 cm (7 inch) round cake tins.

2 Put all the ingredients except the honey,
cheese and chocs in a bowl and fold together.
Divide the mixture into the cake tins and bake
in the middle of the oven. Pierce the middle
of each cake with a metal skewer: if it comes
out clean, the cakes are cooked. Ease out the
cakes onto a wire rack to cool.

3 Use a knife to level off the top of one cake.

4 Mix the honey and 3 tablespoons of the
cheese together and spread the mixture on the
levelled cake. Place the other cake on top and
frost it with the remaining cheese.

5 Decorate the cake with dog chocolates and the
appropriate number of candles. Don't forget
to make a wish as you blow out the candles!

Pests and parasites

Did you know that your puppy will have 'pets', too, if you don't take steps to prevent them moving in? Nasty parasites such as fleas and worms can make your puppy itchy and miserable, or even really ill, so you need to keep them at bay.

Parasite problems

Worming your puppy and applying a flea treatment regularly will help to keep him healthy. If you do neither, these internal and external parasites will thrive while he becomes unwell.

Signs that your puppy may have a flea infestation include agitation and constant scratching, and red and sore patches of skin. Fleas can also cause anaemia.

Roundworms and tapeworms (the most common sorts of worms in dogs) cause all kinds of problems, including malnutrition and gut damage. A thin body with a pot belly is a classic sign of worm infestation, as is your puppy dragging his bottom along the ground as if to scratch it. It's a good idea to worm him a day or two after you bring him home for the first time.

A poorly puppy will not feel much like being cuddled or responding to you, so you really owe it to both of you to keep him free of fleas and worms.

Zap those pests!

Happily, keeping your puppy parasite-free is simple. The best place for you to get advice and effective applications that will kill fleas and worms is from your vet, who will first check over your puppy thoroughly and then prescribe the best treatment for him.

Wormers usually come in tablet or powder form, both of which can be mixed with a little canned meat to make dosing easy.

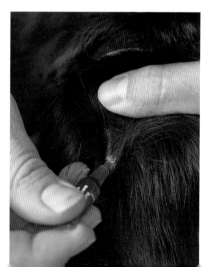

The most effective treatments against fleas are usually available as oral treatments, via injection or as 'spot-on' dispensers. These are treatments which are squeezed directly onto your puppy's skin in an area that he can't reach to lick (such as between his shoulder blades).

No fleas on you

- When treating your puppy against fleas, make sure other canine and feline pets are done at the same time, otherwise there is the risk that re-infestation will occur immediately.

- Vacuuming on a daily basis, paying particular attention to skirting board areas, under radiators and where your puppy sleeps, will pick up fleas and their eggs, helping to keep your house and carpets flea-free. Empty the bag afterwards to prevent eggs hatching inside it and escaping onto the carpet again.

- Washing your puppy's bedding every week or so will kill flea eggs.

Vaccinating your puppy

For peace of mind and to help keep your precious pal in tip-top health, provide your puppy with protection from doggy diseases by getting him vaccinated. Young pups are especially vulnerable to contracting the various nasty canine infections that rear their ugly heads every year.

Deadly diseases

Many vets recommend that puppies are given vaccinations against the four major diseases from which dogs often die if they get them: distemper virus, adenoviral hepatitis, canine parvovirus and leptospirosis. The latter disease is common in rats and transmissible to humans.

Other vaccines are also available, including those against canine parainfluenza and *Bordetella bronchiseptica*. These are both agents associated with kennel cough and are usually required if your puppy goes into boarding kennels or is to be shown.

When to vaccinate

To protect a puppy properly against disease, he should receive two lots of multiple vaccines: the first when he is 6–8 weeks old, and the second when he's at least 10 weeks old. The vaccines must be given 2–4 weeks apart. Your vet will advise you on the frequency of booster vaccinations thereafter.

In certain countries, vaccinations for rabies are given as a matter of course; in others, this is only necessary if you take your dog on holiday abroad, so ask your vet for advice if this is what you wish to do in future.

It's best not to take your puppy out walking until he's fully protected, to prevent him from coming into contact with other animals who may be carrying diseases.

Are there side effects?

Owners' concern about the risks associated with having a puppy (or older dog) vaccinated have increased in recent years. There have been reports of dogs' immune systems suffering due to inoculation with vaccines. It may be inadvisable to vaccinate a puppy if he is:

- ill, when he'll be unlikely to make a good immune response to the vaccine and it may actually exacerbate his condition;
- already receiving a medication that will affect his response to the vaccine.

On balance,
though, many
vets advise that
it's better to have
a healthy puppy
vaccinated than to run the
risks of him not being protected.

Controversy surrounds the
leptospirosis vaccine (which can be
omitted from routine vaccinations if
you wish), as it is this that is most
often associated with an adverse
reaction to vaccination.

First
impressions

Bringing your puppy home

Creating a good impression from the start is key to ensuring your new puppy sees you as his best friend. The way in which you collect him, bring him home and settle him in is crucial in sowing the seeds for a rewarding relationship.

The right time

You and other members of your family need to be relaxed in order to welcome your puppy into your home. If you are moving house or are in the throes of illness, for example, it's better to wait until things have calmed down before getting a puppy.

Your new puppy will need stability for the first couple of days at least so that he feels secure. If possible, collect him the day or evening before you have a couple or more days off work, so that you can devote time to getting to know each other.

Safety zone

Suddenly being transported into a strange new world is very daunting for a young puppy, so you need to make him feel comfortable and safe. It's less hassle, and safer for all concerned, if you transport your puppy home in a secure pet carrier or travel crate. It makes sense to invest in a crate that is big enough to accommodate your puppy

comfortably when he is grown up (and which will also fit in the back of your car).

For easy cleaning after travelling, line the carrier/crate with plastic sheeting and absorbent material, such as newspaper. Provide a snug nest area in a corner using soft bedding such as pet fleece.

Once you've got your puppy home, the crate can also double as his 'den' where he can rest undisturbed and feel safe (see pages 40–41). This way, you do not need to buy a separate bed. A crate will also come in useful for toilet training (see pages 42–43).

Take it easy

You'll be keen to get home, but drive carefully on the way, so your puppy isn't thrown about and learns to associate cars with an unpleasant experience. In case he gets travel sick, take some kitchen roll and a plastic bag to mop up and dispose of any accidents along the way.

Home sweet home

Carrying your adorable puppy over the threshold of his future home and into his new life with you is a great feeling! Puppies are incredibly adaptable and soon settle in, but make this easier for him by following a few simple rules.

On arriving home, put your puppy straight into the garden or yard for a few minutes and praise him when he toilets – this is the first step in toilet training him.

Play a short game with him outside and then encourage him to come back inside. Let him investigate his new home, before you show him where his den is in the puppy area you have prepared in advance (see pages 20–21).

Puppy's den

Your puppy's sanctuary should be in a quiet area of the house to help keep his stress levels to a minimum. Make sure he's got fresh water to drink and a cosy bed to sleep on. A couple of food treats given in his den will confirm that it's a good place to be.

Giving your puppy an activity toy to play with will help keep him busy and happy, taking his mind off all the strange sights, sounds and smells around him. Soon these will be the norm for him.

First steps

Resolve to make your puppy's first few hours and days with you as calm as possible. This isn't always easy if you have excitable children who are desperate to hold and cuddle him all the time (see pages 50–51).

Sleepy puppy

Puppies need to sleep a great deal, so it is a good idea not to disturb your little pal when he's taking a nap. A tired pup is much more likely to become snappy and show 'unreasonable' behaviour.

For the first few weeks, your puppy's time will be divided between eating and sleeping, intermingled with some play. Although it's tempting to play endlessly with him, try to avoid over-tiring him in the early, stressful days when he's still trying to settle into his new environment.

Playing safe

Slippery floors are a real hazard to a puppy, especially when he is racing around, so keep him away from these or put carpet down. Dogs cannot get a grip on polished wooden floors, vinyl flooring or smooth tiles.

It's better to be safe than sorry. To avoid falls, block off stairs with a baby stair gate.

Sleeping arrangements

After a busy first day together, you and your puppy will be in need of a good night's sleep. Here's how to ensure you both have a refreshing rest and sweet dreams, so you are ready to tackle the day ahead in the morning.

All tired out

By bedtime, your puppy will have played himself out and begun to look sleepy. After his last feed, put him in the garden to toilet, praising him when he does so, and have one last quiet wander about.

Then, after a cuddle, tuck him up in his crate (see pages 40–41) with a treat waiting for him, so that he associates bedtime and being left alone with something good. Ensure he has fresh water available in case he's thirsty during the night and a soft dog toy to snuggle up to as a littermate replacement (but make sure he shows no interest in chewing the toy; swallowed fabrics can be fatal). A flavoured chew toy will help to keep him occupied (and stop him chewing the soft toy) if he does wake.

Bedmates

You may wish to keep your puppy in his crate next to your bed for the first week or

so, then gradually move it away so that he is sleeping contentedly in his own area within a month. Being on his own the first night away from his mother and littermates is pretty scary, so your presence will be comforting. Be careful not to fuss him too much: just a gentle word will reassure him if he needs it.

It is best not to have your puppy in your bedroom on a long-term basis unless you intend him to sleep there permanently. Otherwise, he'll come to expect this and may create a fuss when he's not allowed in there.

Wee small hours

If you hear your puppy make a fuss and try to get out of his crate in the night, it's probably because he needs to toilet, so try to get him outside quickly and without fuss. As soon as he's relieved himself, settle him down again.

Avoid picking up your puppy and cuddling him every time he whimpers merely for attention – rather than a desperate need to toilet – and he should be happily sleeping through the night within about a week.

Crate expectations

Training your puppy to use a crate happily is very handy. Also known as a den, puppy pen or cage, a crate serves both as a bed and as a quiet, secure place to which he can retreat when he feels the need.

All-round asset

While a crate may at first seem like a cage, it is useful for keeping your puppy separate from people when he first comes home with you, for toilet training (see pages 42–43) and as a safe place in which to put him to travel. It can also double as a safety zone when you introduce him to other pets.

Once your pup is toilet trained and happy in his new home, you will only need the crate on rare occasions, such as to transport him to the vet.

Make it inviting

It's vital that you introduce your puppy to a crate correctly, so that he sees it as his sanctuary and not a prison cell. Use comfy bedding, toys and treats to encourage him to go in it, leaving the door open so he can go in and out as he wants. The best time to do this is after a play session when he is tired and the lure of somewhere comfortable and peaceful is most likely to work.

Put the crate in a quiet but not isolated area of the house, so your puppy will neither be disturbed nor feel abandoned. Don't place it in direct sunlight, or in areas that get very hot (such as beside a radiator) or very cold (in a draught from an open door or window).

Accustom your puppy to staying in the crate by feeding him there. Bear in mind, however, that puppies generally need to toilet after eating and that dogs are predisposed not to soil where they sleep. If he's left in the crate too long and eventually toilets in it, this could make him unwilling to stay in there again. Leave the door open at all times: shutting your pup in his crate can give rise to behavioural problems.

A good place to be

Giving your puppy an activity toy or treats will help keep him entertained in the crate and he'll view it as a good place to be. Good crate training is about positive reinforcement, so never use the crate as a 'punishment pen'.

Increasing the length of time your puppy is left in the crate should be done while you are at home. Work up gradually from a few minutes to half an hour. You may wish to say a particular word or phrase whenever you put him in his crate. He will soon learn to head for the crate when he hears it.

Once he is used to spending time in the crate, a puppy that is prone to chewing anything he can get his teeth into can be removed from temptation until the behaviour has been resolved (see pages 152–153).

Toilet training

Puppies need to be taught to do what comes naturally to them outside, or in a specially designated area if you live in a flat, *not* on the floors inside. Clever pups are quick to learn this, but you may have to put up with a few accidents at first!

Be prepared!

Until he gains fuller control over his bodily functions, your puppy will need to relieve himself frequently. Put down newspaper so that any messes are easier to clear up until he is toilet trained completely.

Signs that a puppy needs to toilet include pacing the floor, refusing to settle, whining and going to the door. Watch out for him seeking out a quiet corner in which to 'go'. If you do catch him in the act, scoop him up and take him outside.

Outside toilet

A puppy usually needs to toilet after eating, playing and waking up, so take him outside at these times to a designated area, marked off clearly with a length of rope or hosepipe. When he relieves himself there, praise him lavishly so that he knows his actions in that place were desirable. Leave your puppy's last faeces in the 'puppy toilet' to indicate to him by sight and smell that this is the right place to go, but clear up everything else.

Cleaning up

Don't use household cleaners containing ammonia – a component of excretions – to clean up accidents. The lingering smell will encourage your puppy to soil the same spot again. Instead, use pet-stain cleaners.

Toileting tips

- Don't shout at or smack your puppy if he has an accident. He won't understand and will simply become frightened of you.
- Never rub your puppy's nose in his mess: you'll scare him rather than stop him soiling in the house.
- Always reward him when he 'goes' outside, so he learns that this is a habit well worth repeating.
- The longest your puppy should be left in his crate during the day is three to four hours; at night, no more than five to six hours. It is unfair to leave him any longer.

The name game

Deciding what to call your puppy is great fun – there are so many excellent names from which to choose. In fact, it is likely that his name will have pretty much chosen itself the moment you set eyes on him!

Name training

Teaching your puppy his name is easy. Crouch down in front of him, open your arms in a welcoming gesture and call his name. When he comes to you – as he is sure to, out of curiosity – reward him with a treat and lots of fuss. He'll soon come to recognize his name as he associates the sound of it with good things.

Tongue teaser

When choosing a name, it's wise to pick one that is short and rolls off your tongue in just one or two syllables. That way, it's easy to say quickly and your puppy will soon learn to recognize it.

It's also a good idea to choose a name that won't embarrass you when you call him (try a dummy run in the privacy of your home first if you have any doubts). In addition, remember that you want your puppy to learn and listen out for your verbal commands, so avoid names that could be confused with a command – such as Rolo with 'Roll over!'.

Total recall

Once he has learned his name, you also need to teach your puppy to come back to you when you want him to, and not just when he chooses. This is essential for his safety when he is off-lead.

If your puppy knows that coming back to you means he will get a reward, he's more likely to do so. Initially, give him tasty treats (such as small pieces of sausage or cooked liver) or a prized toy; but, as he becomes conditioned to come back to you on command, praise and attention will probably please him just as much.

'Puppy, here!'

Teach recall in a safe, enclosed space, such as the garden, so that your puppy cannot run off and get himself into trouble. Give the command 'Here!' after his name, and when he responds correctly by coming to you offer him the treat or toy. He'll soon get the idea and you can make a game of it, so he quickly learns that coming back to you is likely to be rewarding.

If your puppy doesn't respond, don't get annoyed with him. Simply go to him, let him sniff and taste the treat to regain his interest, and keep trying again until you succeed.

Pleased to meet you!

Your puppy will want to be friends with other household pets, but they may not wish to be pals with him – either because they want to be boss or because they see him as a threat to their safety. Careful introductions are therefore essential.

Making new friends

A crate, food rewards and time are the keys to successful introductions to pets such as cats, caged birds, rabbits and hamsters, for both their and your puppy's safety and sanity. Put your puppy in a crate first to let the pets see, sniff and get used to each other without being at risk. If they get off on the wrong

foot, it will take longer for them to accept each other.

To accustom your puppy to another household creature, put his bedding in its bed or near its cage for a while to transfer the scent, then put the bedding back in his crate. He will learn to recognize the animal's scent and accept it as part of the family.

After the initial introduction using the crate, let your puppy out but keep him under control and see how they fare. Use food rewards to distract him if he becomes excited or frightened, then reward him for being calm. Don't allow him to chase other pets as this can provoke an irresolvable feud.

Top tips

- If you have an older dog, it's a good idea to have someone bring him out to meet the new arrival on neutral ground (such as a neighbour's garden or at the breeder's) before you bring your puppy home. This way, the older dog can meet him without feeling he has to guard his home from an 'intruder', and is therefore more likely to accept him.

- Before you bring your puppy inside, remove all food bowls and toys so that the older dog won't get possessive about them: most dogs won't stand for a strange puppy stealing their things!

- To avoid jealousy, make a fuss of the other dog first, then your puppy.
- Ensure bossing to establish pack hierarchy doesn't get out of hand, and do not allow aggression to develop over a toy or food.
- Don't leave your puppy and older dog alone together until it's obvious they have become friends.

Puppy hugs

A puppy can be so cute that you can't help wanting to pick him up and hug him all the time. But you need to do it right, in a way that is not scary or unpleasant to your pup – then he will love you forever for your care and consideration!

Ready for inspection

It is important to handle your puppy from day one to get him used to being handled all over. A dog generally dislikes having his eyes, mouth, paws, tummy, ears and anal area inspected, especially by someone he doesn't know. However, you and your vet or dog groomer will need to be able to touch and inspect your pet's 'off limits' areas easily if they need attention.

The tender touch

While it might be instinctive to pat your puppy, he'd much rather you stroked him – you'll understand why if you try both actions on yourself! Firm but gentle strokes feel much nicer than hard thumps on the ribs.

Puppies might feel all floppy and soft like cuddly toys, but they don't bounce back after being dropped or squeezed too tightly! It's therefore unwise to let children of six years old or under play with, lift and carry your puppy without supervision. Rough handling, especially by over-enthusiastic children, will make a pup wary of being handled and picked up at all. Particularly undesirable is the fact that in self-defence he may start showing aggression whenever someone tries to approach him.

'Open wide, puppy'

Regular checks of your dog's teeth and gums will help you spot any problems there might be early on. To ensure your dog is quite amenable to having his teeth and gums inspected, make a habit of looking at them on a daily basis. You can train him to respond to the command 'Open wide!', which will be very useful if he ever needs to have his mouth examined by a vet.

Gently stroke your puppy's gums with your fingertips to help him become accustomed to having his teeth cleaned. Use a toothbrush and toothpaste specially made for dogs to avoid 'dog-breath' and help keep his mouth clean and sweet-smelling.

HOW TO PICK UP
AND CARRY YOUR PUPPY

1 Crouch down and gently but firmly gather your puppy to you, with one arm around his chest to keep him from breaking free and the other arm under his bottom for support.

2 Keeping your puppy close to your body, so that he feels safe and secure and can't jump from your arms, stand up slowly.

3 Carry your puppy close to your chest. To put him down, simply reverse the actions. Throughout, bend from the knees to avoid straining your back.

Young pals

Puppies and kids make a great combination: many children count their four-legged friend as their best mate, and research says that children who treat pets with respect and care are likely to do better at school and develop into well-balanced, responsible adults.

Team work

Children have to be shown how to handle and speak to your puppy correctly: always gently, yet firmly. Teach them not to grab at him, especially when he's resting or eating his dinner, or he may snap back out of surprise and self-defence. Because they are often unaware of the possible results of their actions, for everyone's safety never leave young children alone with your puppy, no matter how good-natured he is.

It is important to explain to your kids how scary their behaviour can be to a little puppy. Sit down and discuss with them how they should behave with and around him while he's still tiny and settling into your home.

Fun and games

Children adore playing with puppies, and puppies adore it too! However, keep an eye on them as kids can get carried away and not realize when a game is getting so out of hand that someone could get injured.

Explain to children that they must not carry and run with your puppy in case they fall and hurt their little friend. Educate them to keep play sessions short and sweet, so everyone has fun without your puppy getting too excited and over-tired.

Puppy's little helpers

• Show children how to pet your puppy gently and where he likes to be stroked.

- Ask them to help feed him, and show them how to tell him to sit and wait before he can have his meal.
- Teach them how to tell your puppy what to do and how to reward him for obeying.
- Warn them not to shout at or smack your puppy, because it will hurt and scare him.

Getting kids to help with a puppy's daily care gives them an important responsibility. As well as teaching them the basics of how to look after a pet, such responsibility is good for both their self-discipline and self-esteem. It also builds a great relationship between the two parties.

Think positive

Positive training is far more effective than using punishment or negative techniques, which can lead to behaviour suppression and welfare issues. Your puppy will be much happier for it, and see you as a source of security rather than fear and worry.

Dangers of negative training

Using punishment and other negative techniques, such as physically restraining your puppy or even just ignoring him for long periods of time, can result in him suppressing his natural behaviours and becoming fearful, frustrated and confused. He may develop a feeling of depression and helplessness, where he gives up on ever getting anything right, and this can eventually lead to unpredictably aggressive behaviour. This is obviously not what you want for your pup!

How positive training works

There are four simple steps to successful training using positive techniques:

- When your puppy does something good – for example, toilets outside – reward him with praise and perhaps a food treat to encourage him to repeat the behaviour in the future. This is known as positive reinforcement, because it uses a positive experience (praise and a treat) to 'reinforce' the desired behaviour.
- When your puppy displays unwanted behaviour, don't punish him or tell him off. Such negative action doesn't help and will simply upset him. It can also encourage him to repeat the unwanted behaviour, by

drawing attention to it. If you ignore his mistake, the behaviour is more likely to fade over time.

- Avoid situations where unwanted behaviour is likely to occur: for example, take your puppy outside regularly to toilet so that he is less likely to feel the need to do so in the house.
- Encourage him in a behaviour you do want, rather than preventing one you don't – take your pup outside at frequent intervals rather than shouting at him if he tries to toilet in the house.

Using these techniques to reward wanted behaviours and discourage unwanted ones will help you develop a trusting relationship with your puppy and increase his sense of security and well-being when he is with you.

House rules

Be consistent with house rules and commands. Allowing your puppy to do something one day and then not allowing it the next may result in a confused puppy that displays stress- and anxiety-induced behaviours, such as toileting in the house.

'Play nicely!'

Puppies equal play, and they are so exuberant about it that they make you feel good. But bear in mind that there is a right and a wrong way to play with your young pal in order to keep things sweet and ensure there are no tears before bedtime.

Puppy parenting

Puppies learn through play and it's a crucial part of their development. When they play with other canines they learn how to relate to their own kind, read body language, use their teeth softly, and cope with different breeds and sizes of dog.

Out of their natural environment, puppies need to learn how to fit into family life, so you need to take the place of your puppy's doggy pack members in order to educate him to live in harmony in the human world. So, when your puppy plays with other family members, especially children and elderly people, he needs to learn from you how to be confident but not over-boisterous.

Out for the count

Play-wrestling with your pup seems good fun when he's small, but as he gets bigger it won't be – especially if he grows into a really big boy!

Don't allow your puppy to play-bite. Simply say 'No!' and stop playing with him (see pages 56–57). There are other, more appropriate games that you can play that don't get either of you into scrapes (see pages 86–87).

You should dictate when it's playtime and when it's time to stop, so it's vital to teach him what 'Finish!' means (see pages 52–53). Like human infants, puppies just don't know when to stop playing!

Play plan

Two or three 10- to 15-minute play sessions through the day are better than one long,

exhausting one, and give you both something to look forward to.

Take your puppy's breeding into account when playing games with him. Too much rough-housing or tug-of-war games can over-stimulate some types, especially larger

breeds like German Shepherds and Setters, while chasing games can over-excite others such as Border Collies and Terriers.

Intermingle play with training, so that it's all one enjoyable game to your puppy. Training then becomes a treat, not a chore. Keeping everything interesting and fun will pave the way to creating your perfect puppy.

Play-biting

Puppies love to chew things because it helps them with teething and learning important skills, but it can get painful if it's your limbs your pup gets his teeth into while having a romp! Training him not to do this makes playtime more pleasant for both of you.

Ban play-biting

Play-biting or fighting is part of a puppy's instinctive learning process for hunting and food-gathering. If you want to discourage him from doing it, using positive training techniques to reward him for performing alternative, desired behaviours is a very effective strategy. Do not try to prevent the biting by using punishment or other negative actions, as these will only confuse and frighten your puppy.

- If your puppy seems intent on play-biting, distract him by giving him a command he knows well, such as 'Sit' (see pages 70–71). He can then carry out this desirable action instead of biting. When he sits, remember to reward him with lots of praise and a treat. He will quickly learn that there is nothing to be gained by play-biting, and that alternative behaviours have far more rewarding consequences!

'No teeth' tips

- Handle your puppy's mouth from day one so that he becomes accustomed to hands being in and around his mouth without biting at them.
- Give your puppy toys that he can chew on while playing, so that he has no need to use your hands and arms.
- Don't encourage your puppy to play-bite, and be strict about not allowing children to provoke him into biting them in play.

If all else fails

It may be that you have tried any or all of the strategies described opposite and are still unable to discourage your puppy from play-biting. If this is the case, as a last resort you can try a tactic that uses the same principle as humans do to stop biting their fingernails: you can spray your hands and arms with a non-toxic, bitter-tasting liquid (available from pet stores) that will quickly have your puppy recoiling in disgust when he mouths you. After a number of repetitions yield the same nasty taste, he should have learned that biting humans is likely to be unpleasant.

At your bidding

Teacher's pet

Now that your puppy is happily settled into your home and has learned to respond to his name, the fun can really start. The time is right for you to embark on training him to be the most obedient dog in the world!

Cheeky baby

Like a lively human toddler, your puppy will soon have you running around after him all the time. Letting him do this is not healthy for either of you, so while you must be gentle and kind with him you also have to be quite firm. Otherwise, you'll soon find yourself becoming exhausted by his needs and demands.

In order for him to grow into a well-mannered, housetrained, friendly and obedient dog, your puppy needs to learn, at his own pace, how to be all of these things.

STEP 1

- Name training
- Begin socialization: accustom puppy to household sights and sounds (television, washing machine, vacuum cleaner)
- Begin toilet and crate training
- Begin patience training
- Look into puppy socialization/training classes to start once you reach step 5.

STEP 2

- Collar and lead training
- Continue socialization: have puppy meet people of both sexes and all age
- Begin behavioural training as necessary, such as for play-biting and/or jumping up

Your training plan

The five-step training plan outlined below provides an example of some of the steps needed to start your puppy on his journey to becoming the perfect (and most perfectly behaved) pal. To guarantee that training sessions are effective, keep them short – your puppy will not be able to concentrate for more than than 5–10 minutes at a time. Always try to end the training session on a positive note before your puppy becomes tired out and bored.

STEP 3

Get puppy used to being near animals such as horses and cattle. Don't let him chase them as this defeats the object and you might end up with a 'chaser', a large vet's bill and being sued by the owner of the livestock.

STEP 4

- Introduce car travel
- Continue socialization: once vaccinated, begin accustoming puppy to outside sights and sounds

STEP 5

- Gradually extend car journeys
- Start puppy training/ socialization classes
- Puppy should be going in his crate for time out or to rest in his 'den'

Take it easy

Puppies are funny little bundles of fur with apparently boundless energy and it's extremely tempting to play with them for hours. Just like human babies, though, they tire quickly and can become fretful, so be certain your puppy gets enough beauty sleep and 'time out' to relax.

Patience is a virtue

Naturally, you'll want to spend as much time as possible playing with your puppy and taking him for walks, but don't overdo it. Growing bones and developing ligaments, muscles and tendons can be damaged if placed under too much stress. Being patient will pay off in the long run when you're the proud owner of a fit and healthy mature dog.

Children naturally want to run around when playing with puppies, but an over-excited pup may end up following his instincts and nipping his 'prey'! To avoid this, teach children not to play 'chase' with your puppy.

Puppy patience

Patience is not easy for a puppy to understand. He will be far too busy zipping around, exploring new things. So that he doesn't wear you out within a week, when he asks for your attention teach him to be patient – by encouraging him to perform an alternative action and then rewarding him.

HOW TO TEACH PATIENCE

1 Don't let your puppy demand attention any time he wants it or he'll become a proper little pest, with you and with visitors. If he does want your attention when you are busy, perhaps by jumping up or pawing at you, give him the 'Down!' command (see pages 76–77).

2 When he lies down, sit quietly and count to 3. Don't ignore him, but stay quiet and be patient.

3 Now you can reward him for being quiet, patient and undemanding, by giving him plenty of praise. This way, your puppy will learn that he gets attention when you want to give it and not when he demands it.

'Who's a good boy?'

Puppies respond best to praise and rewards. So, always remember to treat your doggy pal as you'd like to be treated yourself. Being clear and consistent, kind yet firm, when training your puppy will elicit desirable responses, just as it does in humans.

Puppy pleasers

Puppies love to please their owners, and they enjoy this even more when they receive enthusiastic words of praise or a tasty treat. Reward – which can also include a favourite toy, playtime or loving touch – is therefore the key to owning a happy and obedient pup.

Don't get cross

To teach your new best friend how to behave in the way you want him to, always think in terms of kind yet firm, reward-based handling and tuition. Avoid getting cross with your puppy and resorting to raising your voice or even hitting him. Why? Because a dog does not understand the concept of feeling 'guilty' for doing something you don't like or require of him: all he knows is that you are angry with him for some reason he cannot comprehend.

Being aggressive towards your puppy will dent his confidence and, because of fear and in an effort to protect himself, he may react aggressively or defensively. Simply ignore any unwanted behaviour, using distraction techniques or time out when required. This way, he'll soon learn that the behaviour he's displaying is not a rewarding one – it's as simple as that!

Leave the room

If you ever feel you are going to lose your temper with your puppy, take some deep breaths and count to ten while you regain your self-control (and sense of humour!). Leave the room if you have to – just don't take out your frustration on your furry friend, even if he is the cause of it.

Grrrrr!

However, there are times when a 'No' from you – given in a quiet 'growl', while simultaneously turning your attention away from him – is appropriate. This simulates how his mother and siblings would have shown their displeasure when they needed to, so your puppy will know that the behaviour which elicited that response is unacceptable. Take care not to frighten sensitive puppies, as this can lead to self-protective aggression.

Table manners

Every dog owner knows how excited his pet can get at the thought of being fed. In fact, if he can, your puppy will have his nose in the bowl before you've emptied the can into it! Teaching mealtime manners is a good way to bring peace and some doggy etiquette to the proceedings.

I'm starving!

When your puppy is not asleep, he will be constantly on the lookout for food with which to nourish his growing body. Resisting those soulful, pleading eyes can be extremely difficult, and it is tempting to give your puppy more food than he actually needs. Remember that tasty treats and rewards form a part of his diet, too.

You must steel yourself against overfeeding, otherwise your pet will carry more weight than is good for him. As long as he gets the right amount of a well-balanced meal each day, he won't starve.

Feeding foibles

If your puppy is a picky eater, or bolts his food in just a few gulps, it can be a sign that something is amiss. Check the following:

Type of food Make sure your pup has plenty to chew on and a variety of flavours to enjoy, to keep him occupied and avoid behaviour problems due to hunger and boredom.

Feeding frequency Ensure your puppy never gets really hungry by feeding him at least twice a day, and preferably more often. Otherwise, he may become obsessed by food and very protective of it at mealtimes, perhaps even aggressive.

Feed bowls Your puppy may be worried by the size of his bowl (too small or too deep), its material (too shiny) or where it is placed, any of which may deter him from eating well.

Can I eat now?

If you don't want your puppy to mug you as soon set down his bowl, you will need to either occupy him by giving him his meal at the same time, or distract him by offering him a delicious and long-lasting chew to work on. Make sure that everyone in the household sticks to the same routine, so that he feels secure about the mealtime rules.

Begging and stealing

Never give your puppy scraps of food from your plate while you are eating a meal. If you indulge him, even only occasionally, he will soon learn that sitting next to the table

looking at you appealingly can bring a tasty reward. You may find yourself with a greedy pet that begs for food, barks at you while you are eating if you don't give him anything or even helps himself from the table the moment your attention is elsewhere.

Walking on a lead

Walking your puppy on a lead is simple, isn't it? Well, it is if you teach him that it feels good to wear a collar and walk by your side, attached via the lead. Do it right and the pair of you can look forward to enjoyable, controlled walks. Do it wrong and he'll end up pulling you all over the place!

HOW TO WALK ON THE LEAD

1 Hold the lead in your right hand and a reward (treat or toy) in your left, and move it around to get your puppy's attention. Keeping the lead slack, walk backwards and call his name. If he's reluctant to follow, let him mouth the toy or taste the treat, then call him again and continue backing away.

2 Once he's walking towards you, bring your reward hand around towards your left leg and then forward, and he will turn to follow it. Walk forwards, rewarding him as you do so, and using the command 'Heel!'.

4 During initial lead training, keep a toy or treat in your left hand so that if your dog becomes distracted, starts pulling or lags behind, you can entice him back to the correct position and pace, then reward him.

3 This is the correct way to hold the lead and the correct position for your puppy by your side.

Collar your puppy

Initially, it is best to put a collar on only for short periods, praising him lavishly to reassure him. Ensure that it fits well: you should always be able to fit two fingers underneath it. Once the collar is on, try distract your pup with a game or a treat, so that while he gets used to the feel of

something around his neck he also associates it with a rewarding experience.

When he's completely at ease with the collar, clip on a short lead and let him follow you around a little. Give praise and rewards, and when he's happy with that exercise encourage him to walk beside you as you hold the lead.

'Sit!'

Getting your puppy to sit down on command looks impressive to others and demonstrates how well trained he is, but actually it's really easy to achieve and incredibly useful too. All you need is patience and his favourite treats.

Ace result

Having your puppy in the sit position is the starting point for further training exercises, such as 'Stay!' (see pages 74–75) and 'Down!' (see pages 76–77). Four main principles apply to teaching your puppy to sit – and do various other things – on command. The acronym **ACER** may help you remember them:

1 **A**ttention
2 **C**ommand
3 **E**xecute
4 **R**eward

HOW TO TEACH YOUR PUPPY
THE 'SIT!' COMMAND

1 Get down to your standing puppy's level by kneeling in front of him. Hold a treat firmly between your thumb and third finger and let him sniff and taste it, thereby focusing his attention on you and it.

2 Slowly raise the treat above your puppy's head so he has to look up to see it, and give the command 'Sit' – he'll find it easier to sit down to keep the treat in view. If he jumps up, ignore him and patiently start again.

3 As soon as your clever puppy is sitting, praise him lavishly and give him the treat he so richly deserves. Repeat the exercise a few times in every training session, always ending on a success. Practice makes perfect, and remember to keep training sessions short and sweet.

Top tip

It's also amazingly simple to teach your puppy to sit using a hand signal. Once he's got the idea of sitting when you give the command 'Sit!', say the command and at the same time give a hand signal, replicating what you did when raising the treat but extending your index finger. Instantly reward him with praise when he sits. If he has trouble understanding what you want, repeat the treat exercise in steps 1–3 and he'll soon learn what the hand signal means.

'Leave!'

There are times when, for various reasons, you want your pet to leave alone things such as food, other pets, shoes and animal droppings. The easiest and way to teach him to do this is to use positive reinforcement and get him to perform an action he already knows instead.

Food incentive

An extremely effective way to teach your puppy to leave something is to start with food. Begin by having him on a lead and then put down his food bowl. However, do not allow him to eat yet: use the lead to restrain him gently if necessary and instead ask him to 'Sit!' quietly by your side (see pages 70–71).

Wait until your puppy looks at you for permission to eat, even though this may take a little while. When he does, you can say

'Eat!' encouragingly and allow him to do so. Remember to praise him lavishly for being obedient and patient. Make sure that this ritual of giving a command he already knows is repeated at every mealtime until eventually your puppy will wait calmly off-lead until told to eat.

While he is eating, add a treat or two to his bowl so he learns that hands near his food are non-threatening. This way, you are teaching him not to be possessive over items

he regards as his and will avoid problems of aggression in the future.

Once your puppy understands this routine where food is concerned, you can then use the 'Sit!' command to get him to leave other things, whether it is items that he chews or anything else.

Now expand the exercise. While your puppy is waiting to eat, step back from him and use the command 'Wait!' or 'Stay!' (see pages 74–75), which he will do because he is unwilling to move away from the food. Then return to him, praise him and allow him to eat.

Simple and effective

Using these positive training methods, you will be able to teach your puppy quickly and easily to leave things alone, and to stay and wait exactly where you want him, just by giving him a command that he already knows. It's the simple ideas that are always the best!

'Stay!' or 'Wait!'

Getting your puppy to stay where you want him, both indoors and out, is essential. For instance, you can use 'Stay!' or 'Wait!' if you have visitors and want your puppy to remain politely in his bed, or if he needs to stay put for safety's sake while you are out on a walk.

HOW TO TEACH YOUR PUPPY THE 'STAY!' COMMAND

1 Put your puppy into the sit position (see pages 70–71) by your left heel, then reward him for doing so.

2 With the lead slack, give the 'Stay!' command and hold your hand with the palm open in front of your puppy. Repeat the command and take a step out to the side. Repeat it again, then walk all the way around him closely.

3 Reward your puppy and then repeat the exercise, moving a little further away at the front but coming close again at the back, so your puppy doesn't feel inclined to move towards you. Again, reward him well. Whenever your pup moves from the stay, take the exercise back a step and start again.

4 Develop the stay further as your puppy becomes more confident that you are not leaving him and is comfortable with staying put. Extend the lead and increase the distance as you walk around him.

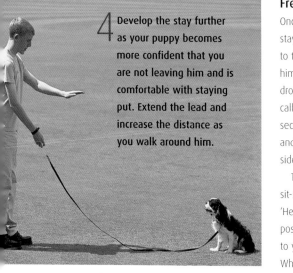

Free to stay, free to go

Once your puppy has learned to stay on the lead, you can progress to the free stay. Move away from him, give the 'Stay!' command and drop the lead on the floor (this is called the sit-stay). Wait a few seconds, then walk back to him and around, finishing by his right side. Then reward him well.

To release your puppy from the sit-stay, call his name and then 'Here!', adopting a welcoming posture to encourage him to come to you. Reward him when he does. What a good puppy!

'Down!'

Teaching your puppy to lie down and stay in that position until you say otherwise is useful in lots of situations, such as when the vet wants to check him over, for grooming and for just having him lie quietly while you are occupied with something else.

It's scary down there!

A dog is at his most vulnerable when lying down, so when you are teaching your puppy to do this it is absolutely essential to offer him an instant reward. Furthermore, you should lavish him with lots of confidence-boosting praise.

Up again

Getting your puppy to sit up and stand from a lying position is easy. Put a treat under his nose and then raise it above his head, saying 'Sit!' or 'Stand!' at the same time. Reward him for the correct response with the treat and praise.

Down and stay

If this is all going well, you could try extending the down exercise into a stay.

Step away from your puppy, saying 'Stay!' as you do so (you can signal as well if you like – see pages 74–75). Wait for a couple of seconds a short distance away, then go back to him and reward him well. You can then gradually increase the distance you put between you and your puppy as you command the stay. You'll be surprised at how quickly he learns this!

Multi-tasking!

Practise the down, sit and stay exercises over and over, until your puppy is clear and happy about each one. Then request a sit, then a down and then a stay, and reward him. Finally, request all of these, followed by a stand after the stay, and then reward him again. This will become a game your puppy really enjoys.

1 With your puppy in the sit position, get him to focus his attention on a favourite treat in your hand.

2 Put the treat under his nose, then slowly move it down to the floor between his front legs.

3 He'll start to sink down to get the treat. When he does, say 'Down!', and when his elbows rest on the ground give him the treat and lots of praise. Once your puppy has learned to lie down on command and is happy there, move on to the roll-over exercise (see pages 78–79).

'Roll over!'

It's extremely handy when your puppy will lie down and roll over on cue. This is a trick that will impress your friends and is also very useful for grooming his underside, checking him over for any lumps and bumps and, of course, tickling his tummy – which he'll absolutely adore!

HOW TO TEACH YOUR PUPPY THE 'ROLL OVER!' COMMAND

1 With your puppy in the down position (see pages 76–77), hold a tasty treat under his nose and slowly move it around to one side. Let him sniff at and lick the treat so that he is keen to get it.

2 Slowly bring the hand that is holding the treat right round. Your puppy will flop onto his side to swivel his head, neck and upper body around, to keep the reward in sight. As he does so, command 'Roll over!' and at this point let him have the treat and praise him well.

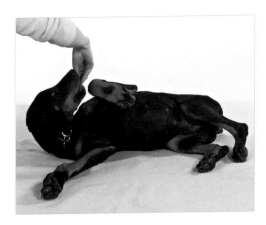

3 Once your puppy is happy in this position, continue by moving the treat further around, letting him nibble at it as necessary to keep his attention, so that he has to roll onto his back. At the same time, say 'Roll over!' and reward him well when he does so.

4 Repeat step 3 until your puppy is completely comfortable with lying on his back. Then move a treat right over and say 'Roll over!', so that he has to roll onto his other side to keep it in sight and gain his reward. Give him the treat and lots of praise.

Easy does it

Exposing his tummy makes your puppy vulnerable, so he will only roll onto his side or back when he feels safe and secure. You won't achieve a successful result unless you are both relaxed and at ease with each other.

Some breeds, such as Greyhounds and Whippets, find it more difficult than others to roll over due to their physique, so take this into account – if your puppy is one of these, only ask him to go as far as he is comfortably able.

'Go to bed!'

When you want your puppy to move away or leave you alone, it's vital that you give him somewhere pleasant to go. His bed is the obvious choice, and the command to send him there comes in handy at times, such as when you don't want him near something.

Treat training

Use your puppy's favourite treats to teach him this exercise: those that are really smelly and tasty usually do the trick! Hot dog sausages, cut up into small pieces, and liver treats are both good. Put the delicious morsels into a plastic container, show them to your pup, let him sniff them and give him one to whet his appetite for more reward.

Using the command 'Go to bed!', guide your puppy to his bed using the treat box and then reward him. Reinforce this with a 'Stay!' command (see pages 74–75), reward again and place a chew toy next to your

puppy, so that he will be even more reluctant to leave his position. This way, he'll come to learn that his bed is always a good place to be.

Continue with whatever it is that you want to do while your puppy is away from you. If he comes to you without being called, simply repeat the exercise, using the 'Go to bed!' command as you put him back in his bed and reward as before.

Key points

- Keep the exercise short to start with so your puppy doesn't become bored and switch off.
- At first, try not to wait too long before calling him back to you, otherwise he'll get bored or become anxious and come looking for you.
- If your puppy comes back to you uninvited, ignore him at first. After a short while, return him to his bed, again using both the 'Go to bed!' command as well as the rewards.
- Practise this exercise often so that your puppy will learn by reward association that 'Go to bed!' is a good command to obey, and therefore is happy to do so.
- Always finish your training on a positive note, so that your puppy remembers it as a pleasant experience. This method of training is very simple but also extremely effective in achieving the desired response.

'Fetch!'

Chasing after a toy is one of a puppy's greatest pleasures. To save you from having to run after him to retrieve it every time, just so you can throw it for him again, play it clever – get him to bring it back and give it to you!

HOW TO TEACH YOUR PUPPY THE 'FETCH!' COMMAND

1 Holding up your puppy's favourite toy and wiggling it about will excite him as he senses a game is about to begin.

2 Once he's focused on the toy, throw or roll it away and say 'Fetch!' at the same time. Your puppy is sure to go to it.

3 When he's picked it up, encourage him to return to you by adopting a welcoming posture and saying 'Fetch!' again in an excited, happy voice. If he drops the toy and returns to you, simply walk over to it and encourage him to pick it up and bring it to you.

4 When your puppy does bring you the toy, at first don't take it from him straight away. Instead, make a fuss of him and then offer a treat, saying 'Give!'. To take the treat, he'll let you take the toy without fuss. Praise him again and then repeat the exercise.

Give it to me

Use a toy that your puppy can carry easily and you can take from his mouth without risking your fingers. Suitable toys include a Kong, a rubber ring, a ragger (rope toy) or a rubber tugger (tug toy). From the start, teach your puppy to give you the toy when he returns, rather than just drop it. Then, if you ever want to do obedience competitions with him he'll already be trained to retrieve and give as required.

Hand signals or cues

Have you ever wondered how some owners control their dogs as if by magic, just by moving a hand in a certain way or adopting a particular posture? Well, that's because these owners have taught their dogs to respond to hand signals. It's easy when you know how!

How to speak 'dog'

Unlike humans, dogs cannot speak in order to make themselves understood, so they mainly use body language to communicate with each other. Because of this, sometimes it's difficult for your puppy to understand what you want of him just from your voice commands and tone.

If you've had a bad day at work or are feeling a bit poorly, you may sometimes unwittingly use a tone of voice that causes your puppy to imagine you are cross with him. Remember that puppies always respond best to kindness and reward, and a sharp or cross word from you can set back the confidence-building and training work you've done so far, by denting his feeling of safety and security in the most important person in his world – you.

Teaching hand signals (also called hand cues) at the same time as you give voice commands is one way of avoiding this potential problem. It's also a great way of training deaf dogs. It's vital, though, that other members of your family learn to use the same hand cues (and voice commands) as you, so that your puppy doesn't end up totally confused.

Hand signals and voice commands

'Watch me!'

'Over!'

'Sit!'

'Close!'

'Down!'

'Here!'

'Stand!'

'Stay!'

It's playtime!

'Do you want to go out?' and 'Do you want to play?' are questions
your puppy will be ecstatic to hear every day once he discovers
what they mean. Both are guaranteed to make his ears prick up
and his tail almost wag itself off.

Fun and games

Puppies are great fun to play with. Always
exuberant and happy, their favourite part of
being your pal (apart from being fed!) is

when there's entertainment to be had.

Puppies love walks and games – both
together is even better! Games on a walk,
varying the route daily if you can, help to

keep your puppy interested and focused on you. Games are part of successful training, and help to prevent him becoming distracted and wandering off.

In addition, playing games with your puppy is a brilliant opportunity for you both to learn to communicate, trust, have fun and work together.

Game plan

There are lots of games to play, including:

Hide and seek Crouch down behind a bush or tree and call your puppy to find you.

Treasure hunt Hide toys and treats for him to find (see pages 182–183).

Follow the leader Make a simple obstacle course of cones and other items to go under, through and over, and see how long it takes you and your puppy to negotiate it.

Find it Line up empty containers in a row and put a treat under one. See how long it takes your puppy to find the jackpot.

Playtime tips

- Wait at least forty-five minutes after feeding before exercise and play. Running around on a full tummy is not good for either of you. Another good time is before your puppy is due to be left alone for a

while, so that he'll sleep contentedly when you are gone.

- Old slippers and shoes are not appropriate toys for a puppy, otherwise he'll think all your footwear is fair game.
- Avoid using sticks and lumps of wood as toys – splinters can cause injury, while a stick can spear him. Stones are out too, because they can break teeth and are easily swallowed.
- Two or three short play sessions a day are much better for your puppy's growing body than one long one.

Clicker training

Using a clicker to help with training is a brilliant concept, since it provides an instant cue to reward desired behaviour offered by your puppy. It's not hard to learn how to use it correctly: practice makes perfect!

Instant gratification

A clicker is a small hand-held tool comprising a plastic box with a metal tongue inside. When pressed with the thumb, it makes a distinctive double-clicking sound. Small enough to hide in one hand, a clicker is simple to use and very effective: just press and click to 'condition' good behaviour.

The great thing about the clicker is that it is instantaneous: the exact moment your puppy displays a required type of behaviour, click, then reward him with a treat. He will soon get the idea that this sound means that a particular type of behaviour is wanted, and this is reinforced by the reward. Click, reward; no click, no reward!

Another good thing about a clicker is that you can use it at a distance, and your puppy will come to you for his expected reward. Invaluable at the start of training, the clicker can be phased out once a certain kind of behaviour has been learned.

Be on time!

Accurate timing is the key to success. Practise without your puppy until you can use the clicker with pinpoint accuracy. Test yourself by throwing a ball into the air and clicking before it hits the ground, or throwing it against a wall and clicking before it reaches its target.

To implement clicker training, you'll need some tasty treats. Begin the association with the clicker and a reward by throwing down a treat and clicking just before your puppy eats it and returns to you. Click once only and don't hold the clicker close to your puppy's head or ears. Repeat several times.

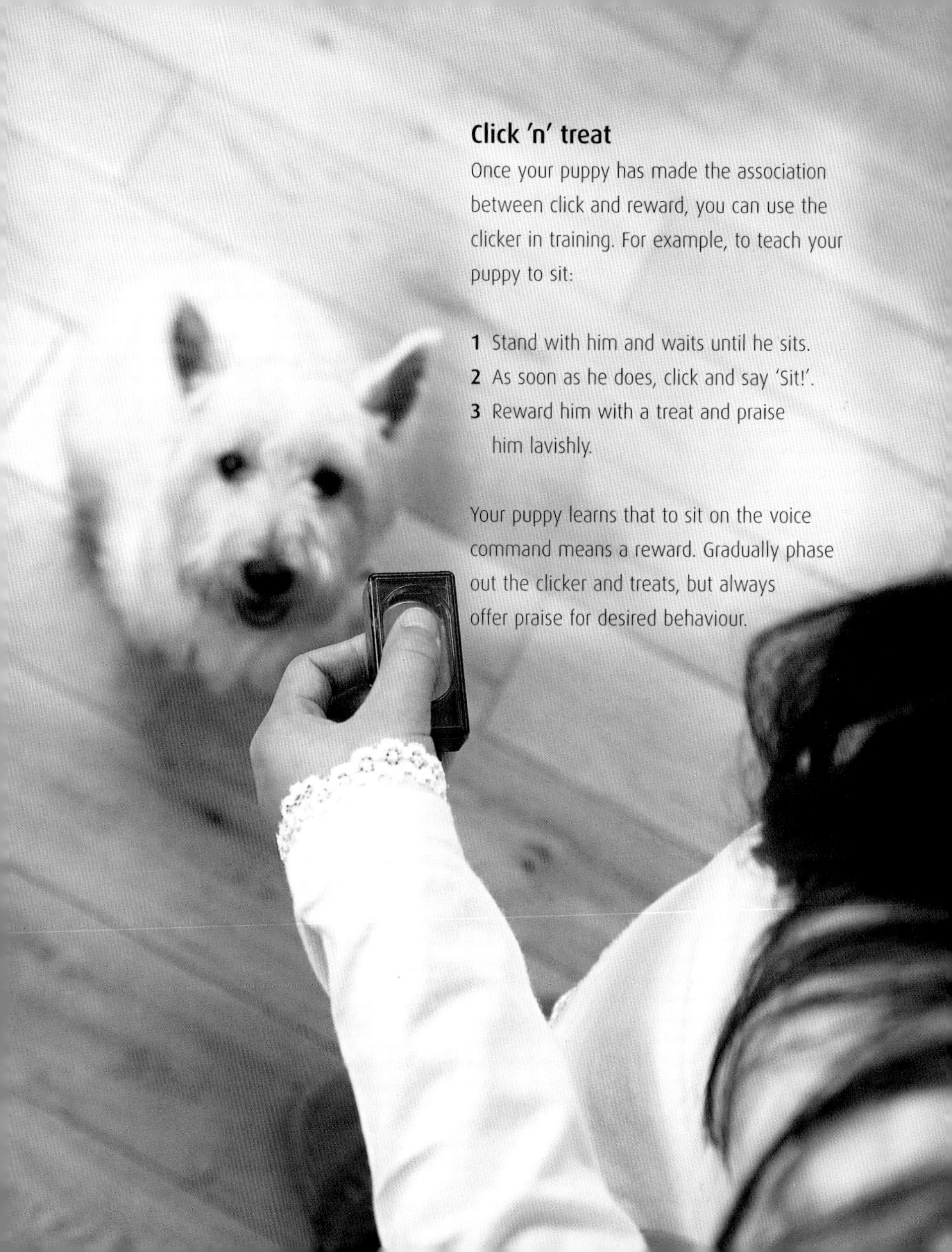

Click 'n' treat

Once your puppy has made the association between click and reward, you can use the clicker in training. For example, to teach your puppy to sit:

1 Stand with him and waits until he sits.
2 As soon as he does, click and say 'Sit!'.
3 Reward him with a treat and praise him lavishly.

Your puppy learns that to sit on the voice command means a reward. Gradually phase out the clicker and treats, but always offer praise for desired behaviour.

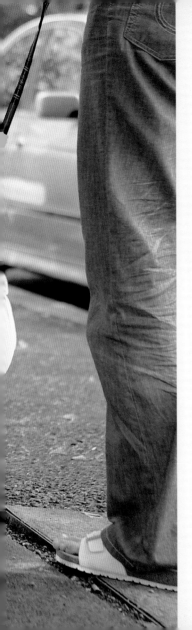

Puppy meets the world

Sights and sounds

Imagine you are in a world of giants and noisy machines, and are not sure if they intend any harm towards you. This is what awaits your puppy in the outside world, so you need to teach him there's no need to be afraid.

'That sounds scary!'

For you, your home is a comfortable and safe place to be, but in the early days your puppy may well find the unfamiliar household sights, smells and sounds very scary indeed. Noises from the telephone, television and

washing machine can send him into a panic the first time he hears them, especially since canines have a more acute sense of hearing than that of humans.

Acclimatizing your pet to accept these everyday things is quick and easy once you know how (see also pages 122–123). The crucial socialization period for a puppy – when he is naturally at his most curious and willing to explore – ends at around 18 weeks of age, although there are variations depending on his breed and character. It is important to introduce your puppy to as many new things as possible before he reaches this age.

Situation normal

Initially, keep your puppy in a different room while using household machines and distract him with an activity toy (see pages 16–17 and 134–135) or food. This way he will associate the noises with good things and learn that they pose no threat.

Soon you'll be able to let him into the room with the items and he'll take no notice of them, as he is acclimatized to their sounds. For example, a vacuum cleaner can appear to be a noisy monster, but if you let your puppy investigate it while it's running but stationary then he'll learn, at his own pace, that it won't hurt him. If you remain unconcerned, he'll soon accept household noises as the norm.

Streetwise

Outside, you need to introduce your puppy to traffic and people everywhere, from busy streets and markets to 'trick-or-treaters' paying a visit on Halloween (see pages 96–97 and 170–171). Do this gradually, until he views it all as perfectly normal and nothing to be bothered about. Make sure his collar is tight enough so that he can't slip from it should he take fright and try to bolt.

Car journeys

It's lovely to be able to include your puppy in everyday life and there's nothing more pleasant than a family outing to the park or beach. For many, this involves a trip in the car, so you'll need to accustom your puppy to travelling.

Safe passage

Creating a pleasant association with riding in a car is the best way to help your puppy become a happy traveller. This doesn't mean just taking him to the vet and back, when your puppy might learn that going in the car means an unpleasant experience awaits him!

The safest way to transport your pup is in a crate – ideally his den, which can double as a travel crate, so he's in his familiar, safe environment. This will also prevent him from distracting you while you are driving, and helps to keep him safe and secure in the event of an accident. Put in some non-slip

flooring, such as a rubber mat, with his bedding on top.

Alternatives are a strong pet carrier (for a small puppy) or a dog grille. You can also buy a canine travel harness, but this is not ideal for a puppy.

Precious cargo

Keeping the car well ventilated is essential, as is driving with consideration. Ensure that your gear changes and cornering are smooth and braking gradual, so your puppy isn't flung around in his crate. Motion sickness can also be aggravated by jerky and erratic driving. Remember that smooth driving produces less sick!

At first, take your puppy on short journeys – just around the block to start with. Reward him for going in the crate and again at the end of the journey, then gradually extend the journey time.

Trip tips

- Never leave your puppy unattended in the car, even while you just pop into a shop. Dogs can become overheated in a short time, which is potentially fatal.
- To avoid him vomiting, don't feed your puppy immediately before a trip, although he can drink. In an ideal situation, it is

best to wait several hours after feeding before travelling.

- Encourage your puppy to toilet before a journey.
- Take water and a bowl with you on trips.
- Pack plastic bags, kitchen roll, rubber gloves, cloths, water and pet-safe disinfectant so you can deal with any sickness or toileting accidents.

Meeting new friends

Your puppy will love meeting people and getting lots of attention
– as long as he's confident around them and secure in the
knowledge that they pose no threat to him. It's your job to help
him learn to be this way.

Getting together

In much the same way as you enjoy meeting
friends and sharing experiences with them,
your puppy is likely to be no different. He
will prize meeting up with familiar friends
at the local park, on walks and at training
classes, and having the opportunity to chase
around and play together. As you meet up
with other owners and their puppies, both
you and your pup will look forward to
socializing and enjoying their company. If
you are new to the area, consult the

internet, local press or your vet surgery to find details of a local training or dog-walking group you can join.

Pleased to meet you!

Try to expose your puppy to people of both sexes, all ages and different appearances to get him accustomed to meeting and being with all sorts, and reward him so that he views their company as a good thing. For example, people arriving at the door in uniform or a motorcyclist in his leathers and helmet can be a bit scary for a pup, so it pays to introduce him to such sights. Ask the people you meet to give him attention and food treats (carry some specifically for this purpose), so that he views them as rewarding.

People overload

A word of warning, however: don't try to introduce your puppy to too many people at once or he may become overwhelmed by it all. Do it gradually, over a period of time, so he becomes accustomed at a steady pace he can cope with mentally. Ten minutes per day is enough to begin with. Time and patience works wonders, and remember that socializing is an ongoing process throughout your puppy's life.

Grabbing your puppy

One thing you should get your puppy used to is being grabbed suddenly. There are bound to be times when someone will do this to him, especially if he meets young children or when you or someone else needs to get hold of him quickly for safety's sake. Practise grabbing hold of him unexpectedly, but then reward him immediately so he learns that this is nothing to be alarmed about.

Puppy classes

Puppy socialization classes are equivalent of human nursery school. Here, your little friend will make new pals of people and other puppies, and learn how to meet, greet and play with them in a controlled and safe environment.

Find the right trainer

Once your puppy has been vaccinated and lead trained (see pages 30–31 and 68–69), the best way to begin to socialize him is to take him to tailor-made classes run by a reputable trainer.

Word of mouth is the best way to find a trainer – for example, ask your puppy's breeder if they can recommend anyone. Before taking your puppy along, ask if you can go and watch a class to ensure it meets with your approval. A good trainer won't refuse this reasonable request.

If the class is held inside, take note of the flooring: it should be non-slippery to avoid accidents. Any training should be done using reward methods only.

No bullying

At a class, your puppy can meet others of his own age and size, as well as their owners. Allowed to intermingle – first on the lead, then loose – the puppies will quickly find an acceptable level of chase and play, and sort out the pecking order among themselves.

It is important in these initial stages that a puppy isn't forced into a frightening situation.

A good trainer will ensure that any play-fighting doesn't get out of hand and will prevent any bullying.

Puppy 'parties'

Puppy parties usually cater for puppies aged between 10 and 12 weeks; older pups go on to puppy training classes. It's best that no more than two or three puppies of a similar age, character and size are allowed to play with each other at any one time, to avoid bullying or a shy puppy being overwhelmed by more outgoing ones.

Parties that take place at veterinary clinics, which are usually run by the nurses, also provide an ideal opportunity for puppies to meet the staff, and furthermore have the added advantage that the pups come to really enjoy being there, instead of associating the sights and smells of the surgery solely with injections and other unpleasant or frightening experiences.

Nanny dogs

Contact with adult dogs is needed too. Some trainers have their own well-trained dogs for this, who like puppies but will not accept rough play. 'Nannies' such as these will teach your puppy respect for his elders without becoming aggressive.

Going to the vet

A puppy that likes going to see the vet will take the tension out of such visits for you both in future. Here are some guidelines on how to make a trip to the clinic more of a pleasure than a pain, whatever the reason for the visit.

Getting the basics right

You will need to register with a vet and clinic with which you feel comfortable. Visit several clinics if possible, to find the one you are happiest with. Look for clues when you go – if the vet or staff seem dismissive of you and uninterested in your puppy, go elsewhere. If you are not at ease, your anxiety will transfer to your puppy as soon as you go in and he'll sense there's a reason to be scared.

When you visit the clinic with your puppy, careful and considerate driving is essential (see pages 94–95) or he'll associate going to the vet with an unpleasant experience.

For your own peace of mind, it's a good idea to take out pet insurance or put money

aside regularly for vet's bills, both routine and unexpected.

Relaxing your puppy

Always reward your puppy when at the vet's, so that he associates the visit with something good. Take treats and his favourite toy to distract him while you are waiting, and stay calm yourself so he senses everything is fine and there's nothing to worry about. Ask the vet and staff to make a fuss of your puppy, so that he views them as friendly and good to be around.

It pays to pop into the clinic on a regular basis just to say hello, not only for treatment, so that your puppy doesn't view each trip there with suspicion. Many clinics encourage this, as it is easier for them to deal with a calm and relaxed puppy than one who is stressed and frightened.

Party time

Dogs who haven't been 'vet trained' generally don't enjoy visiting the vet. This is usually because they only visit when they need some sort of treatment, which more often than not is uncomfortable or painful. It's therefore a good idea to take your puppy to puppy parties at the vet clinic (see pages 98–99), so that right from the start he views it as a good place to be, associating it with play, toys and treats, and friendly staff who make a fuss of him.

Boarding kennels

At some point, perhaps when your puppy is a little older, you will be looking forward to going on holiday – and so will your puppy, provided you've arranged five-star accommodation where he'll have as great a time as you!

A1 accommodation

There may be times when you feel you have no choice but to put your puppy in boarding kennels. You may worry that he'll be unhappy while you are away, but the chances are he'll have a fantastic time – as long as you've chosen a reputable establishment. There's no doubt, however, that he'll be delighted to see you again at the end of his stay.

Kennel search

The best way to find a suitable kennel is by word of mouth. Ask dog-owning friends and relatives, and your trainer, if they can recommend somewhere. Alternatively, look on noticeboards at your vet clinic, grooming parlour and pet store. Lastly, check the local press, telephone directory, library and internet.

The next step is to visit to check out the place (see opposite). Bear in mind that good kennels get booked up well in advance, so don't leave all this until the last minute.

Puppy motels

Many humans like to be pampered on their holidays, and they might feel that their animals deserve a similar standard of service. Some kennels offer such home comforts as armchairs, music, central heating, home-cooked cuisine and even supervised access to a heated doggy swimming pool! While such places will be more expensive than regular kennels, you may decide that knowing your puppy is living in the lap of luxury while you are away warrants the extra cost.

Check 'em out

Visit all the kennels on your shortlist to see if they meet your standards. In their turn, most kennels insist on up-to-date vaccinations and will want to check your puppy's certificate. Kennels should:

- be clean;
- be licensed by the local authority, with the certificate on display;
- employ friendly, dog-loving, helpful staff.

When you visit, make sure that you ask for details about the following.

- Cost per day and what this includes.
- Exercise arrangements.
- Kennel policy if your puppy is taken ill while you are away.
- What insurance cover is in place should your puppy escape and get lost, become injured or, in the worst-case scenario, die while in their care.

Understanding your puppy

Talking 'dog'

The better you are able to understand what your puppy is trying to tell you, the happier he will be and the better will be the relationship between you. Developing a good knowledge of 'dog speak' will enrich your lives together in many rewarding ways.

Understanding each other

No matter how hard you try, or how intelligent he is, your puppy will never fully understand the language you speak. The only language he will ever 'speak' is 'dog', which consists primarily of behaviour and body language. He can, of course, learn the meanings of some of your verbal commands and will constantly be trying to communicate with you in ways other than speaking.

Your puppy uses all his senses to work out what's going on. His behaviour is a reaction to this assessment, but don't forget that he is seeing things from lower down, smelling things more strongly and hearing things from much further away than you.

Watch and learn

To develop your understanding of what your puppy is saying, you can make a point of observing him as he communicates with other dogs. You'll instantly see that they 'talk' to each other using mainly body language, so the position of the tail, general posture, demeanour and expressions of the ears, eyes and mouth are all crucial. Puppies try to communicate with humans in the same way, so it's important that you know what that wagging tail (see pages 110–111) and other body language signs really mean.

Happy or sad?

As a general guide, a happy and confident puppy will look relaxed, hold his head up, keep his tail straight and may wag it in pleasure. His ears will be pricked and his mouth and jaw will appear relaxed.

An unhappy dog withdraws into himself. He may also develop what you consider undesirable behaviour, like stereotypies (obsessive behaviour), in an effort to comfort himself.

Some puppies become stressed by the hectic pace of their owners' lives, so take care that you are not too busy to meet your puppy's needs. Be aware also that actions or a tone of voice conveying impatience will wound him deeply, causing unhappiness.

Above all, knowing your puppy's personality is the key to recognizing his emotional state, and responding accordingly is the secret to happiness.

Happy chappy

How do you know if your puppy is happy? And how can you tell if he likes you? Learning to understand what your puppy is 'saying' to you is important in developing a great relationship with your four-legged friend.

Puppy language

Puppies generally love everyone and are happy to meet and greet new friends, whether they are human or animal. Your puppy communicates by means of body language, posture, facial and vocal expressions, and behaviour. Once you have learned to recognize these, they will tell you about his emotional state.

Just like us, puppies experience a full range of emotions from happiness and contentment to depression, frustration, fear, anxiety, anger and aggression. As your relationship with your puppy develops, you'll know what mood he is in just by looking at him. This way you'll be able to work out how he is feeling, what he wants and what he needs in order to provide him with a great life.

Happy puppy

A happy puppy is confident, calm and relaxed. He looks well in himself, doesn't constantly seek attention, shows no behaviour problems, has a good appetite and generally appears a picture of health.

Puppies have different personalities. While one happy pup might be playful, energetic and curious, another – equally happy – may be more laid back, quiet and less exuberant. You'll soon learn whether your puppy is the energetic type or not!

Does he like me?

If he thinks you are simply the best, your puppy will be relaxed in your company, happy to receive fuss and attention from you, and willing to interact when you want to play with him. If he doesn't like you, he will be wary and avoid you – in which case you need to learn how to make things right between you.

BODY LANGUAGE

Generally, you can tell from the way your puppy carries himself and his behaviour what message he wants to convey to you. For example:

Aggression, fear and/or uncertainty	Stiff stance with jerky movements, snarling/growling, tail tucked between his legs
At ease/content	Relaxed posture, smooth movements
Calm and alert	Kind, interested expression, ears pricked
Frightened	Hunched up, ears down, cowed expression, growling or whining
Unhappy or ill	Stiff posture, ears down, slow movement
Submission	Crouching, licking his lips, whining
Playful/happy/ attention-seeking	Relaxed body and tail wag, 'smiley' face, ears lolling, excited yapping/barking

Waggy tail

Your puppy's tail is a barometer that can help you to gauge his state of mind. You might think that when a dog wags his tail he's doing it because he feels happy or pleased to see you, but this isn't always the case.

Social signals

Puppies usually start wagging their tails at about 6–7 weeks old. This is when they are first starting to learn social skills and enjoy play – tail wagging can often amount to waving a white flag if playtime ends up getting a little rough!

Tail wagging can also be the equivalent of a human smile or handshake, as well as a sign of excitement or pleasure – perhaps as

you approach with your puppy's lead to take him for a walk. However, tail wagging can also be a warning, or a sign of aggression or defensiveness.

Your puppy will only wag his tail at things he wants to communicate with and that he thinks will respond to him. A good example is when you approach him with a bowl of food: he wouldn't wag his tail if he simply walked into the room and found a bowl of food on the floor.

Watch the wag

In some circumstances, perhaps when meeting an unfamiliar puppy or adult dog while out on a walk, tail wagging can mean your pup is insecure and worried. To read his body language effectively you will have to learn to observe his tail position, look at how he's wagging it, and also take into account the circumstances and any other signals your puppy is presenting.

No tail at all

Studies show that puppies with docked tails (surgically removed for fashion) can be at a social disadvantage. One reason for this is that they are unable to communicate with each other effectively, as other puppies and adult dogs cannot read their tail position.

TAIL POSITIONS

Happy and friendly	Tail up, wagging confidently from side to side
Playful	Tail wagging with a relaxed body, 'smiley' face, lolling ears
Curious	Tail up, possibly slow, uncertain or irregular wagging
Uncertain/insecure	Tail low between legs, hesitant wagging

Afraid	Tail low between legs
Aggressive	Tail up or straight out from body, maybe fluffed up, possibly wagging
Predatory	Tail straight, low and still (so as not to alert prey)

Keeping your puppy content

Having a puppy is a two-way process. Your playful puppy will bring pleasure into your life and help to make you feel more content. In return, you will need to do all you can to make his life just as happy and each day full of fun.

Have some respect

There's a lot to learn about ensuring your puppy is the most contented canine in town, but it's worth knowing you have done everything possible to keep your puppy brimming with joy and good health. Even better – it doesn't take a great deal of time, money or effort!

The key to having a contented puppy is to consider his feelings, just as you would respect human family members' and friends' feelings. Whatever your emotional state, try to put your puppy's first and don't let your actions or tone of voice convey impatience, since he won't understand why this is being directed at him. Learning how to be unselfish about fulfilling your puppy's needs, both mental and physical, is the first step in learning to respect him – and then he'll adore you all the more.

Rules of respect

Approach Avoid sudden movements or loud noises directed at your puppy which he might construe as aggressive, although teaching him to be 'grabbed' is advisable (see pages 96–97).

Understanding If your puppy displays natural behaviour, such as rolling in other animals' faeces or sniffing under other dogs' tails, don't reprimand him. Simply distract him with a toy or food treat.

Companionship To deny your puppy human company for long periods is unfair and can lead to problem behaviour.

Safety Don't put your puppy in hazardous or uncomfortable situations, such as around uncontrolled, potentially aggressive dogs.

10 STEPS TO HAPPINESS

1   Give your puppy a routine and stick to it.

2   Make his life interesting with toys and games (see pages 138–139).

3   Keep that puppy-dog curiosity by hiding toys and treats for him to find.

4   Vary the route of his walks, and try some new activities together as he matures.

5   Keep his coat well groomed and flea-free.

6   Teach him to do jobs, such as find his lead or fetch his dish.

7   Provide him with his own comfy bed.

8   Ensure he has the correct food and enough of it, plus a constant supply of fresh, clean water.

9   Check him over every day for lumps and bumps and signs of illness (see pages 120–121).

10 Tell him what a beautiful puppy he is every day!

A pup's-eye view

Imagine how unhappy your life would be if every time someone stared at you it made you feel afraid. Your puppy needs to be able to look at you directly without perceiving that your gaze is threatening, so spend time practising this on a daily basis.

Eye contact

You can learn a lot from your puppy's eyes and his willingness to look at you.

In the wild, when one dog stares at another he is issuing a challenge. As a result of this, some dogs are so uncomfortable making eye contact with humans that they will begin to lick their lips or pant. Sometimes, more worryingly, eye contact may trigger a sudden aggressive response reaction in a dog who has not been socialized to make eye contact with humans from puppyhood – a case of 'I'll get you before you get me!'.

To avoid this scenario, and so that you and your puppy can look at each other in mutual adoration, it's vital you teach him that eye contact with humans is nothing to be scared of and is actually a rewarding experience.

Gaze praise

Teaching your puppy to make eye contact from an early age without viewing it as frightening or aggressive is especially important if you have children in the house, as they'll often be at his eye-contact height when playing with him on the floor.

Learning that eye contact is good will help to increase your puppy's confidence. Instil this by spending time playing with him each day, giving him affection and food treats while at the same time encouraging him to look at you. When he does, praise and treat him lavishly. Soon you can dispense with the treats and just use praise: your kind voice alone will be more than enough reward.

'Watch!'

It can be very useful to get your puppy to focus his attention on you at any given time. To teach this using clicker training (see pages 88–89), every time you want him to look at you give the command 'Watch!' and as soon as he looks at you click and offer him a food reward. With practice, he'll learn to look at you on the verbal cue alone.

Facial expressions

As you'll discover, your puppy has a whole range of facial expressions to indicate his mood and that he'll use to communicate with you and other dogs. Here's how you learn whether your dog's puckering up for a kiss or pursing his lips in puzzlement!

Watch his mouth

Regularly observing your puppy's expressions in play, or when he's feeling scared or threatened, can give you a good insight into his state of mind, particularly if you also take into account his other body language signals and the situation he's in. By picking up on your puppy's expressions early on, you can learn how to gauge how he is feeling and how to become adept at defusing potentially tricky situations.

A puppy's muzzle, whiskers and neck are sensitive, so be careful when stroking him in these vulnerable areas.

Understanding expressions

Happy Your puppy will have his mouth slightly open and may be showing part of his tongue.

Curious He will generally keep his mouth shut, perhaps cock his head to one side, prick his ears a little and look towards whatever has attracted his interest.

Listening Your puppy will stand or sit still with his mouth shut and ears pricked, trying to work out what it is that he has heard.

Submission Crouching and licking his lips or yawning indicates 'I'm only little, please don't harm me!'

Worried If your puppy has his mouth clenched tightly shut and is turning his head away from something he's seen, he is feeling insecure and worried. This is a pacifying gesture rather than an aggressive one.

Anxious If your puppy is afraid, he'll lower his head and pull his ears back. His lips will be loose or pulled back.

Threatening Your puppy will curl his lips back to expose his teeth and gums. He will often do this after other, more subtle, signals – such as looking away – have failed.

Aggressive A puppy that opens his mouth, wrinkles his nose and exposes all his teeth is giving a final warning that he is about to bite.

Smiley puppies

Some breeds, including Dalmatians and Dobermanns as well as many Terriers, are actually known as 'smilers', as they often greet their owners with their mouths slightly open, exposing the incisor and canine teeth. This is not a sign of aggression, but a submissive gesture.

'I'm unhappy – please help!'

When happy and healthy, puppies are naturally inquisitive, playful and interested in their surroundings. If this does not describe your pup and you think he's unhappy, you'll need to be a doggy detective to discover the cause and then provide a pick-me-up to perk him up.

Is he sick?

An unhappy puppy will sleep more than usual, appear uninterested, withdraw into himself, be reluctant to socialize, and be especially destructive or display aggression. He may also refuse to eat, pant, whine, growl, bark excessively or be over-dependent on you. The first thing to do is take him to the vet to rule out a physical cause.

Soothing scent

If the vet gives him the all clear, a depressed and anxious pup may respond to a dog-appeasing pheromone (DAP) diffuser, available from many vet clinics. DAP is a synthetic version of a substance released by lactating bitches a few days after they have given birth, designed specifically to calm and reassure puppies.

Common causes of unhappiness

Boredom Often seen in breeds that need to be kept busy and occupied, such as Terriers and Collies.

Remedy Keep your puppy occupied and his mind stimulated. See '10 steps to happiness' on page 113.

Anxiety Can be caused by living in a multi-dog/pet household, over-dependence on you or a fear of loud noises.
Remedy Provide an area to which your puppy can retreat and feel safe. A DAP diffuser (see opposite) can be effective too.

Remaining unneutered As your puppy reaches sexual maturity, he/she may become unhappy and frustrated if not allowed do what nature intended, which is mate and breed. Entire (unneutered) dogs are liable to wander off in search of a mate, exhibit sexual behaviour and perhaps become aggressive due to frustration.
Remedy If you don't intend to breed from your puppy, have him/her neutered (see pages 126–129).

Environment A small toy breed or one that loves family life will be very unhappy if excluded from human contact for long periods, or if made to live outside. Conversely, a longhaired breed may find a heated home uncomfortable and prefer to be outside.
Remedy Choose your breed carefully (see pages 10–13). Limit the time your young puppy spends alone.

Puppy health checks

As you get to know your puppy, you'll learn to recognize whether he's fit and healthy or lethargic and unwell. It's important to notice whether he's perky or poorly so that if necessary you can take take him to the vet for treatment.

Signs of distress

It's worrying when your puppy isn't well, but the sooner you recognize this the better his chances of becoming healthy and happy again soon. Indications of illness are unusual behaviour, altered appetite or demeanour, distressed whining, increased or decreased thirst, straining on defecation or urination, vomiting or diarrhoea. Note whether your puppy displays any of these signs so that you can inform the vet, to help with speedy diagnosis and getting the appropriate treatment.

A poorly puppy

Subdued, frightened or miserable demeanour; cloudy or runny eyes (pupils widely dilated in bright light can indicate blindness); dirty, smelly ears; scurfy, flaking or scabby skin with evidence of parasite infestation; open sores; constant scratching (indicated by the action or by red, inflamed areas on the skin); soiled anal area (with evidence of diarrhoea); umbilical hernia (swelling on the midline of the stomach); swollen abdomen (can indicate worms); dirty and unkempt or dull and 'staring' coat; stiff or lame movement; constant whining.

A perky puppy

Alert, curious demeanour; bright, clear eyes; clean nose (a slight clear wetness is normal); glossy, clean coat; clean, supple skin free from scurf and parasites; clean ears that do not smell (test hearing by making a sound out of your puppy's field of vision to see if it registers); clean anal area; no lumps or bumps (especially on the navel); clean teeth and pink gums; normal bodyweight; flat abdomen (unless your puppy has recently eaten); quiet, even breathing; free and easy movement.

Swift diagnosis

A puppy suffering from a digestive upset can soon become dehydrated, as his little body will quickly lose moisture and essential salts and sugars (electrolytes). It's absolutely imperative that he receives veterinary attention within a couple of hours if his ailment hasn't cleared up. If his condition worsens during these first couple of hours, consult a vet sooner.

VITAL SIGNS

Temperature	38.1–39.2°C (100.5–102.5°F)
Pulse	62–130 heart beats per minute – the smaller your puppy, the faster the pulse
Respiration	10–30 breaths per minute – smaller dogs breathe faster

Scaredy pups

Just like some people, some puppies are more shy and retiring than others and can take a while to come out of their shell in a new home. But watching your shy boy blossom under your loving care is one of the best feelings in the world.

Act normally

Generally, a puppy is nervous because he has not been socialized adequately from an early age, so going into a new home is pretty scary and he'll take time to adjust. Allow for this, but don't over-compensate – just act normally and he should soon learn that no big, bad ogres are coming to harm him or eat him up.

Send out relaxed signals – such as yawning or slow blinking – to your nervous

puppy, and don't stare at him even if he's looking to you for reassurance. Ignore him if he gets anxious and behave as calmly as possible so that your body language tells him 'It's all fine, there's nothing to worry about.'

It's a good idea to take your puppy to socialization classes as soon as possible (see pages 98–99).

'Be brave'

Give your puppy a den (see pages 36–41) that he can retreat to for 'sanctuary' and let him come to you, and other family members and visitors, in his own good time. Once he accepts that your home is a safe place to be, and that the humans in his life are friendly and kind, he'll relax, start to enjoy himself and gain in confidence. Tempting your puppy to come to you, other family members and visitors by offering him tasty treats and his favourite toys will help to break the ice, encourage interaction and teach him how rewarding humans can be.

Scenting success

To ease anxiety and help your pup feel good, get a DAP diffuser (see page 118). This can calm puppies frightened of loud noises. Desensitization CDs (found in pet stores) can also help your puppy get used to sounds that scare him. If he shows extreme fear of loud noises, have his hearing checked in case he's hypersensitive to noise.

'Calm down!'

Puppies are full of fun, and some are more exuberantly playful than others. In fact, your puppy can keep you on the go so much that he'll still be asking for more when you are begging for mercy! Here's how to strike a happy balance.

Fun and games

If you don't provide your puppy with enough exercise and play, his natural instincts will drive him into sourcing these activities for himself. Unfortunately you might not appreciate his efforts: what he thinks is fun and pleasurably diverting may well be what you consider to be unacceptable, destructive and bad mannered.

Recognize the signs

It is normal for a puppy to seek your attention, but if he develops behaviours such as chewing household items or occasionally chasing his tail it may be that he isn't getting enough exercise and mental stimulation from you. Do not punish such behaviours. Instead, spend more quality time each day exercising, playing with and devoting attention to your

puppy, thereby channelling his energies into constructive behaviour that's rewarding for you both.

If your pup begins to pester constantly for attention, regularly becomes over-excited (hyperactive), and develops obsessive behaviours such as repeatedly chasing his tail or pacing up and down, consult your vet.

Play and learn

Developing a routine to avoid this isn't difficult. Just set aside some short periods of time each day to play games with your puppy. Little and often is the key, so the games remain fresh and exciting for both of you. Always end on a good note before your puppy becomes over-excited.

You can intersperse the games with brief training sessions, making them rewarding for your puppy so he'll look forward to them. This will help to make him a much more contented and obedient pal.

Keep your puppy safe

Puppies love to explore and find new things, so short walks will satisfy this desire without stressing his immature body. Playing in your garden can be fun, too – but avoid games that put pressure on his joints, such as racing after thrown toys and jumping.

If your puppy looks tired when you are out walking, stop to rest him before carrying on. Don't get into the habit of carrying him home, though: you could regret this later!

Reaching puberty

It's inevitable that your sweet little ball of fluff will grow up, and as he does so certain changes take place in his body. It helps to understand what these changes are and when they happen, so you are prepared for your puppy reaching puberty.

Growing up

To generalize, at 20–24 weeks (around 5 months old) your puppy will be the equivalent of a 10-year-old child. Smaller breeds develop more quickly than larger ones, which take longer to mature due to their size (up to around 14 months of age).

At this age, hormonal changes start taking place in your puppy's body as he prepares himself to do what nature intended – become a parent himself.

As he reaches sexual maturity, it is likely that your puppy may display behaviour you don't consider polite. Some examples of this are: mounting people's legs, trying to escape in order to find a mate, showing aggression and scent marking (sometimes inside the house).

Six-month cycle

On reaching puberty, a female puppy will start to come into season (this is known as oestrus, also called 'on heat') and when she does be ready for mood swings, odd behaviour, and urination or soiling in the house. She may also try to mount other puppies or soft toys. Her season will occur every six months and last 21 days, during which she will discharge bloody fluid from her rear end (vulva).

Unwanted suitors

When a female comes into season, you are likely to find male dogs loitering around outside your house. This is because your puppy's body is releasing chemicals known as pheromones that indicate her sexual condition. Naturally, this attracts canine suitors from far and wide, and you'll have a job keeping her away from potential mates.

Family planning

During a female puppy's season, she will only allow herself to be mated 10–14 days into her season, when the bloody discharge turns clear. This is the only time she is likely to conceive if mated.

There are tablet or injection options for birth control and preventing oestrus respectively, but there are health drawbacks to both treatments and they are not 100 per cent effective. An anti-testosterone drug can be given to males, but again is not always effective. Surgical neutering (see pages 128–129) remains the safest and most effective way of preventing unwanted behaviour and pregnancies.

Neutering

Unless you specifically wish to breed, having your puppy neutered early helps prevent many problems from developing as he (or she) reaches sexual maturity. It is a myth that growing puppies benefit from reproducing: what your pup doesn't know, he (or she) won't miss.

Breeding discontent

On reaching puberty, entire (unneutered) puppies will feel stressed, aggressive and frustrated, and constantly want to roam. They will be at risk from certain illnesses (see below). Furthermore, your pup won't be any happier if you allow him to breed or her to have a litter of puppies.

In the past, males and females were neutered at around 6 months of age, but now both procedures can be done at 8 weeks.

Benefits of neutering

Males

- Removes the sexual urge and the risk of wandering.
- Certain types of aggression are reduced.
- Reduces the risk of hormone-related diseases, as well as anal and perineal cancers.
- Eliminates the risk of testicular cancer.
- Significantly reduces the risk of prostate gland problems.

Females

- Prevents unwanted pregnancies.
- Eliminates any problems associated with her seasons, not to mention the mess!
- Prevents the urge to go in search of a mate.
- Unwanted attention from male dogs is no longer a problem.
- There is a decreased risk of mammary, uterine and ovarian cancers, and neutering helps to prevent uterine infections.

SPAYING (BITCHES)

Before spaying: the female reproductive tract: with ovaries, Fallopian tubes and womb (uterus).

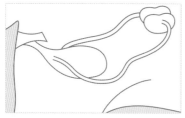

After spaying: the ovaries, Fallopian tubes and womb have been removed.

CASTRATION (DOGS)

Before castration: 2 testicles are connected to the penis via the spermatic cords (vas deferens).

After castration: the testicles and part of the spermatic cords have been removed.

What neutering involves

Males (dogs) are castrated: both testicles and part of the spermatic cords are removed. Females (bitches) are 'spayed': the ovaries, Fallopian tubes and womb are taken out. Surgery is performed under anaesthetic, with stitches closing the wounds. Non-soluble ones are removed after 10–14 days. Most puppies go home the same day. Any discomfort, usually minimal, is controlled with medication.

After neutering

Exercise your puppy on the lead for two weeks after the operation to minimize boisterousness, which could hinder healing. Keep bitches quiet for another few weeks before full-paced play is resumed, but males should be fine after two weeks.

You are unlikely to notice a personality change, although generally his behaviour will become calmer and more reliable.

Body talk

By now you should have a good idea of what your puppy is saying to you from the way he moves, looks, acts and sounds. It's like having the door to a wonderful new world opened for you and your pal, and it makes life together so much easier.

Puppy postures

Here are pictured some typical behavioural traits and actions your puppy may display, with explanations of what they mean.

On the side

Cocking his head to one side is your puppy's way of turning his ears so that he can pinpoint the direction and source of the sound more precisely.

High five

Many puppies learn that lifting a paw to someone, or even pawing or nosing at a person is a guaranteed way of getting attention or a treat. The puppy's head comes up and his senses focus on whatever it is he's trying to get, indicating confidence and determination. On the other hand, a puppy that lifts his paw but with his head lowered (indicating his teeth are out of action) is being submissive.

Fright sight

This young German Shepherd is frightened. If a puppy commonly displays this posture, he will need a good deal of confidence-building in order to make him more emotionally them anxious, frightened and withdrawn. By being sensitive to your puppy's emotional needs and looking after them, you'll help him to feel safe and secure and he'll become a happier dog.

Upside down

Rolling on his back, exposing his tummy and leaving himself vulnerable, displays a puppy's acceptance of a higher-ranking individual, whether human or animal. This strategic positioning is a good one to get the puppy out of a situation in which he would otherwise receive punishment: after all, how could you be cross with such a cutie? Another dog will think: 'Huh, what a softie. He's not worth bothering with because he's no threat to me!'

stable and able to enjoy life. Some dogs, including German Shepherds, are particularly sensitive to their owners' actions, tone of voice, emotions and moods, and raised voices and emotional disturbance can make

Etiquette in the home

'Be good!'

While your puppy is small, you feel you can forgive him anything because he's so appealing. Nevertheless, you'll have to resolve not to let him have everything his own way in the house, otherwise he'll end up bossing you and your visitors mercilessly!

'Mine, all mine!'

A cute and cuddly puppy pretending he's a big bad wolf and trying to be fierce is really funny – but it won't be so amusing when he's mature and displaying those characteristics when you try to take a toy from him or approach his food bowl while he's eating.

So, resolve to nip these potential problems in the bud while your puppy is small, and teach him from day one that allowing you to take toys from him without protest and people to be near him when he's eating is rewarding. Do this by giving him treats and then some fuss when he relinquishes a toy, and by adding tasty titbits to his food bowl while he's eating (see pages 72–73).

Training visitors

While it's important not to let your puppy get into the habit of greeting visitors by jumping up and pestering them for attention, it's equally essential that visitors do not undo all your good training (see pages 142–143 and 146–147) by encouraging him to display such unwanted behaviour and inviting him to play boisterously with them.

Tactfully advise your visitors how you would like them to behave around your puppy, making it clear that rough play is banned and explaining why. If they don't comply, then it's best to remove your puppy from the room. Put him elsewhere with an activity toy, such as a stuffed Kong (see below), to keep him happily occupied until your visitors leave.

Stuff a toy!

Stuffed Kong toys are brilliant boredom-beaters that will keep your puppy safely occupied and quiet for ages while you get on with other things. Simply fill the Kong with unsalted cream cheese and push biscuit treats down into it. Seal in the cheese by smoothing it down with the flat side of a knife and give it to your puppy to enjoy.

Home alone

Although you want to spend every waking moment with your gorgeous puppy, you need to prepare him for those times when he'll be left alone. And yourself for that matter – it'll be a wrench to leave him, but just think how good the reunion will be on your return!

Make it easy

It's vital that you accustom your young pet to being left on his own for periods of time, because there will inevitably be occasions when you do have to leave him home alone. However, there are ways you can make this easier on him, and on yourself.

From the beginning, leave your puppy alone in a closed puppy-proof room for short periods. Start with a few minutes and then gradually build up to longer periods, bearing in mind his toileting needs. Don't make a fuss before you leave or when you return. Aim to make this a normal part of his day, and then he will be happy to be left alone when necessary, such as when you have to go to work.

An independent puppy

For your puppy to remain happy both mentally and physically, being at home for hours on his own while you and your family are out and about is not ideal. If you have to be out all day, try to find a way around the problem. Some owners employ a dog sitter or walker to come in during the day to exercise and play with their puppy. If you are lucky enough to have obliging neighbours, why not ask them to look in? Other owners drop off their puppies at boarding kennels or with dog sitters on the way to work and pick them up on the way home.

Top tips

- Leaving a radio playing low while your puppy is on his own provides him with the comfort of background noise.
- If you know you are going to be out longer than your puppy is used to, arrange for someone he knows and likes to pop in to take him out to toilet and give him some attention.
- Leave your puppy with a stuffed Kong toy (see page 134) to give him something constructive – and non-destructive! – to do while you are out.
- Get your puppy used to going to kennels or staying with a dog sitter (see pages 102–103), to provide an alternative when you are going to be away from home for long periods of time.

Boredom and mischief

Dogs are highly intelligent, so it's important to keep your puppy's mind stimulated so that he doesn't find things to do that you probably won't appreciate. Working and Terrier breeds are particularly predisposed to making their own entertainment if left to their own devices for too long.

'Let me entertain you'

While you don't want to over-tire your puppy with too much mental and physical exercise, too little is just as bad. There are lots of ways to keep him mentally stimulated that don't involve a huge time commitment from you, and just a few minutes each day will make a big difference to your puppy's outlook. The key is to introduce variety and mental challenges that he is physically capable of tackling and will actively enjoy. Your reward will be a puppy that is happier and a pleasure to own. If he's content, so will you be.

10 WAYS TO KEEP YOUR PUPPY HAPPY

1 Match walks and training sessions to your puppy's capabilities, gradually increasing them as he gets older. A tired puppy is a grumpy, unhappy one!

2 Give your pup's toys names and teach them to him. Make a game of asking him to fetch them for you one at a time (see pages 82–83).

3 Make use of interactive toys that are filled with food and dispense treats as they are moved around during play (see pages 134–135).

4 Hide treats and/or toys around the house and garden (where your puppy can get at them easily) and encourage him to find them.

5 Give your puppy 'occupational therapy' with various toys of different shapes, types and textures.

6 Keep one or two favourite toys as 'special treats' and use them as rewards for good behaviour.

7 Cardboard boxes and used (clean) thick plastic bottles make great toys for your puppy to play with. Hide treats in the box for him to enjoy finding and playing with or eating. Avoid highly-coloured boxes where the printing may be toxic though, and remove bottle tops which may be easily ingested.

8 Build a sandpit for your pup to dig around in.

9 Daily grooming will keep him smart and happy.

10 Keep telling your puppy how wonderful he is!

Doors and doorways

Stepping over or around your puppy when he's lying in a doorway or across a passageway can be inconvenient at times. If you want him to learn to move away when required, here's an easy and effective method that uses commands he already knows.

Clear exit

If your puppy is not already lying or standing in the doorway, take action to avoid him doing so. As you get up from your seat, give your pup the 'Stay!' command, which tells him what to do (see pages 74–75). Don't set him up to fail by asking him to remain there for too long. If he breaks the stay, never scold him – simply put him back into position and try again. Always reward him when he does well.

If your puppy is already lying or standing in the doorway, do not step over or around him. Instead, ask him to move using the 'Go to bed!' command (see pages 80–81).

'Shut the door!'

Teaching your puppy to shut the door behind him when he pushes through into a room is very handy. The smaller he is, the harder this trick will be for him though – so it's often best to wait until he's a little bigger and strong enough to attempt it.

HOW TO TEACH YOUR PUPPY TO SHUT THE DOOR

1 Train your puppy to touch a target with his nose. Use a plastic container lid as a target disc. Present it to him and reward him when he touches it. When your puppy will run to touch the target when shown to him, put it against a door at his nose height and reward him for touching it. Introduce the command 'Shut the door!' as you place the target for him to touch.

2 Progress to leaving the door slightly ajar before presenting the target and voice command. Encourage him to run to the target, so that he nudges the door shut with his nose. Reward him with a really tasty food treat and lots of praise. Gradually leave the door further open so that your puppy has to push harder to close it, until he learns to do it by command only. Always reward him well when he succeeds.

Door-training

Inquisitive, full of fun and eager to greet visitors or go out for a walk, puppies soon learn to make a dash for the door if they sense entertainment in the offing. Teach your pal to be patient at these times, not pushy.

Patience

A puppy that pushes past you and rushes to the door when someone calls soon becomes a pest. Not only could this behaviour cause an accident if you trip over him, but people may well become reluctant to visit if they know there's a good chance they will be jumped all over when they enter the house.

Use the reward container technique (see pages 80–81) whenever someone comes to the door. Your puppy will soon learn that going to his designated place when visitors knock is more rewarding for him than rushing to the door to greet them. Eventually, this becomes a conditioned response and you will only need to use treats occasionally – verbal praise will be sufficient the rest of the time.

HOW TO TEACH YOUR PUPPY TO GREET VISITORS

1 To teach door courtesy, your puppy needs to know how to sit and stay on command (see pages 70–75). Then enlist another person to help you door-train him. When the 'visitor' comes to the door, tell your puppy to sit and stay before you open it.

2 Greet your visitor and tell them to ignore your puppy until you call him over. Don't wait too long at first, because if he breaks the stay it may set training back. If he approaches without permission, don't scold him – simply ignore him until he settles and then reinstate the sit-stay.

3 Let your visitor greet your puppy while he's in the sit-stay and then reward him, but ignore him if he rushes over or jumps up. Once he's been greeted, you can either let him stay with you both or tell him to lie down quietly, giving him an activity toy to keep him occupied. Constant reinforcement of this exercise will soon teach your puppy that rushing to the door is not at all rewarding, while not doing so results in pleasant interaction with guests.

'Don't push me!'

Your playful pal is quick to figure things out and will soon realize that when you pick up his lead it means one of his favourite things – a walk! However, keen though he is to explore the great outdoors, he needs to learn that being first in the queue just isn't on.

Who's walking whom?

First of all, teach your puppy to sit and stay (see pages 70–75) while you put on his lead. Always reward him for doing this, initially with treats, then with verbal praise alone. This way, he becomes conditioned to waiting for you to lead him out of the door, rather than him taking you for a walk.

Sometimes, though, an over-confident and exuberant puppy may take the initiative and insist on pushing his way past you to get to the door first. If this happens, you need to take steps to show him that his barging behaviour won't get him anywhere, whereas being a polite puppy will.

Teaching a pushy pup to wait while you open the door and then inviting him to follow you is the next step.

Teach your puppy not to push

Put your puppy on a lead and stand by the door. Tell him to sit and stay while you open the door a little way. If he stays, reward him, then open the door wider and invite him to follow you with a 'Here!' command. If he doesn't stay where he is and attempts to push past you, simply put him back where he was, tell him to sit and stay, and repeat the procedure.

Practise this a few times, until your puppy stops trying to make a break for freedom but instead remains put, quietly watching and waiting to see what you are going to do next. This shows he has learned that pushing past you means he ends up where he started and does not get to go for his walk.

Reward good behaviour

Next, tell your puppy to sit and stay as you open the door. When he does, reward him lavishly. He's learned that waiting is more rewarding than trying to push past you. Now you can tell him 'Here!', and off you go to enjoy a well-deserved walk.

'Don't jump up!'

Your puppy loves you and you love him, but he needs to know that keeping his feet firmly on the ground when he says hello is the best greeting he can give you, and that bouncing up and down at you is not the way to win attention.

In your face

In the wild, dogs instinctively greet returning pack members by sniffing and licking at their mouths to try to get them to regurgitate or drop food. Since the mouth is a rewarding area of the body, your puppy will jump up at you in an attempt to reach it. You need to teach your little pal that this behaviour is unacceptable in the human environment.

A little puppy jumping into your arms may seem truly adorable, but imagine how you'll cope with such behaviour when he is fully grown! Even if you don't mind him almost knocking you over as he plants two paws on your shoulders, if he gets into this habit he could pose a real danger to other people, especially children and the frail or elderly, when out on walks and when visitors call.

Ground rules

Training your puppy to keep his paws to himself is easy, as long as you are insistent and patient with him.

This is easier if you ask someone to help you. If your puppy jumps up at them, tell them not to scold him but instead give him the 'Sit!' command (see pages 70–71). If he sits but then quickly jumps up again, have the person repeat the command. When your puppy makes no further attempt to jump up, the person should then reward him with lots of praise. This teaches him that jumping up means he simply ends up back where he started, while not doing so results in plenty of fuss and attention.

Practise this exercise at home and on walks, until when someone approaches your puppy he makes no attempt to seek attention from or jump up at them. Many people, especially children, love to say hello to a sweet little puppy when out walking, but it's important that you ask them to refrain from doing so until he sits and waits quietly for attention. Also make sure visitors know and follow your rules for giving your puppy attention, and tell them exactly what to do if he jumps up at them.

'Off the furniture!'

Soft chairs are comfortable and you sit on them, so your puppy may decide that he wants to curl up on them with you, too. However, you must resist those baby brown eyes appealing for a cuddle on your lap if you don't want your suite decorated with dog hairs.

In the hot seat

If you'd rather not have your puppy sit on furniture, set a precedent early on and don't ever let him do it in the first place. Undoubtedly, he's a cute little chap and – particularly if he's a rescue pup – you may feel he deserves special privileges while he's still little. However, if you've allowed him to do this, as he grows he'll think it's his right to get on the furniture whenever he likes and may even object if you try to move him. It's not unknown for an owner to end up sitting on the floor while their dog is sitting pretty on the sofa, because they are too afraid to get him off it!

By invitation only

If you want your puppy to sit on your lap or beside you, but only when you ask him to, you need to set clear rules by teaching him that the only time he's allowed on the furniture is when you are there and invite him to do so. It's important that not just you, but all family members, and visitors too, adhere to your rules, otherwise your puppy will become confused about what he is and isn't allowed to do. If you don't want him on your knee while you are sitting down and he approaches with that intention in mind, say 'No!' firmly and be sure he obeys, then reward him for the right behaviour.

Antisocial climber

If your puppy climbs on furniture when he's not been invited to do so, lift him down, saying 'Off!' at the same time, and put him firmly on the floor or in his bed. When he stays there, reward him and tell him he's a good boy. This way, your puppy learns that climbing on furniture uninvited is unrewarding, while remaining off it is much more pleasant. If he's persistently sneaky and jumps up on chairs and other furniture while you are out of the room, get into the habit of putting obstacles in the way to prevent him from doing so.

Barking and yapping

Puppies bark for all sorts of reasons, from tiny yaps to great big bellows, depending on their size and breed. Unfortunately, some love the sound of their voice so much it can drive you, and probably your neighbours, to distraction.

Barking training

Any puppy will bark to sound an alarm to his pack (human or animal) and warn off what he perceives as a threat. With training, however, your pup can be taught not to bark when inappropriate or for prolonged periods.

Bear in mind that simply telling your puppy to be quiet doesn't work, because there is no incentive for him to obey. In fact, he learns that barking is rewarding because you are paying attention to him – and in his mind even being told off is better than no attention at all.

Friends not foes

Your puppy will view your home and garden as his pack's territory. While you want him to alert you to unwanted visitors, barking at everyone who comes to the door or walks past the house can become a real nuisance.

Introducing your puppy to any milk and post delivery people who come regularly will teach him they are friends, not foes – getting them to say 'hello' to him and give him treats is a good idea, and may help to prevent or cure a problem.

Accustoming your puppy from day one to the sound of the doorbell and knocks at the door without him creating a fuss is also a must. As with jumping up, do this by ignoring him when he barks and rewarding him when he doesn't.

Blanket barking

Puppies need to learn that
barking at anything and everything
is unrewarding. When he barks, put
him out of the room or bring him indoors,
and totally ignore him. When he's quiet, give
him attention or a treat, and put him back *in
situ*. He'll soon learn that creating mayhem is
not nearly as rewarding as being quiet. Keep
him where he can't see passers-by and out
of the garden at peak pedestrian times.

Chewing things over

Your inquisitive puppy will love to chew: it's all part and parcel of him growing up. Getting his teeth into items helps to satisfy his curiosity about them, as well as helping him teethe. This is fine – as long as he only chomps on things he's supposed to!

Preventative measures

A puppy that chews things he shouldn't can soon cause a lot of damage to your home, so you need to teach him what he can and cannot chew. Until he learns that your belongings are off the menu, never leave things lying around that you don't want destroyed. Chewing gives your puppy a lot of pleasure, particularly if he is bored, so keeping him positively employed and stimulated is the best way to keep your home intact (see pages 138–139).

Fit for purpose

Chewing is pleasurable for your puppy, so provide him with alternatives to the things you don't want him to chew that will be just as rewarding for him and more acceptable to you. This will teach him that he can only chew certain items that you give him for that purpose. Old shoes and slippers are not suitable, because otherwise he'll think that any footwear, old or not, is fair game.

If necessary, reinforce that certain items (such as shoes) are unpleasant for him to chew by spraying them with a non-toxic anti-chew liquid. This liquid tastes so horrible that after the first bite your puppy won't be keen to go back for a second try and will instead wander off to find a toy that is much nicer to mouth.

Instead, give him chew toys and food chews, available from pet stores. Once they start to break up, replace them so that he doesn't swallow bits that could make him sick and cause internal blockages.

The taste test

If your puppy has already embarked upon his version of 'home improvements', restrict him to an area where he can't do any damage when you are unable to keep an eye on him. Provide him with chew and activity toys to keep him occupied, such as a filled Kong (see pages 134–135) and a ragger. Teaching him to chew these items will take his mind off table legs and other unacceptable items.

Problem behaviour

From time to time, your puppy may display behaviours that you regard as a problem. Instead of telling him off or even punishing him, it is far better to deal with these situations through positive training – by getting him to perform a desired action instead.

Consistent and positive

No doubt you will want to spoil your puppy because he's 'only little' and, of course, extremely sweet. But you won't do him any favours in the long run by encouraging behaviours – such as jumping up in excitement whenever you appear – that you later want him to drop. Such inconsistency will simply confuse him and damage the trust between you. Using punishment and other negative training techniques will have a similar effect. To encourage him to see you as a source of security and comfort rather than fear and worry, use positive training methods instead.

Evasive action

So how can you use positive encouragement to prevent problem behaviours arising in the first place?

Let's say you want to avoid your puppy rushing past you to the front door whenever the bell rings, because this leads to him jumping up at your visitor as soon as the door is open. First, enlist the help of another person to ring the doorbell. Now, instead of allowing your puppy the opportunity, tell him to 'Go to bed!' (see pages 80–81), which is something he already knows how to do. Always reward him when he does well.

After some practise, your puppy should learn to associate the sound of the doorbell with going to his bed. You will then only have to use the command when he forgets!

Resolving problems

Positive methods can also be used to resolve the problem situation should it occur. So, if your puppy does jump up at you or another person, tell him to 'Sit!' instead. When he does so, reward him with one of his favourite toys. This will both distract him from his original idea of jumping up and, in the long term, train him so that he no longer even considers performing the unwanted behaviour. This way, you both end up happy!

Begging for food

There is something rather off-putting about a pair of eyes boring into the back of your head while you are enjoying a meal, so don't let your puppy hound you for titbits from the table. After all, he wouldn't appreciate you pinching food from his plate!

Scrap happy

As well as being a bad habit, begging for food when people are eating can lead to fussy eating (see pages 158–159), so this is not behaviour you want to encourage. If you want to give him suitable food scraps when the meal is finished (avoid spicy food and poultry/small bones), put them in his food bowl as part of his daily ration rather than giving them to him by hand.

Deterring begging

Puppies are natural scavengers, so if there's any food about your puppy will be first in the queue for it, unless he's taught otherwise. There are several things you can do to train your puppy not to beg.

- Remove your puppy from the room while you are preparing food and eating meals, or put him in his crate. You could use a baby stair gate to separate him from the kitchen/dining room, so that he can't get at the table but can still see what's going on and doesn't feel excluded. Giving him his meal at the same time, an activity toy filled with treats or a chew to play with will help keep him pleasantly occupied.
- Resolve not to give in to your puppy's pleading expression and soulful eyes.

Instead, remove him from the eating area or, when he's trained to do so, command him to go away and lie down quietly (see pages 80–81).

- When your puppy has learned to respond to being sent away to lie down and stay, do this every time you, the family and visitors sit down to eat. Ensure that everyone in the household is aware of and abides by the rule of not giving your puppy human food titbits, since this will encourage him to beg.

Fussy eating

Always on the lookout for food to satisfy his rapidly growing body's constant demand for nourishment, your puppy will probably eat whatever is put in front of him. But what if your young friend starts turning his nose up at his meals as he gets a bit older?

Human food tastes better!

Puppies that are given human food seem to prefer it above all else. This is because dogs are instinctive scavengers, and also because this is what their human families eat.

What appears to be fussy eating can often go hand in hand with a pet that is allowed titbits from the table. If he's getting table scraps, other titbits and lots of treats as well as his daily ration, his appetite may not be as keen and he'll opt for the tastier human food rather than his dog food diet every time.

If you give your puppy freshly cooked chicken or steak as a treat, then he may expect it next time and refuse to eat dog food, hoping for chicken instead. If you are soft-hearted and give in to his demand, you'll set this feeding pattern in place.

Poorly puppy?

In rare cases, fussy eating can indicate an underlying medical problem. If your puppy suddenly starts to refuse food, and he's not getting additional table scraps or too many food treats that could explain this change in behaviour, then he could have developed an allergy to the brand of dog food he's being given, especially if he displays any or all of the following symptoms:

• Diarrhoea
• Vomiting
• Skin ailments
• Itching
• Poor coat condition
• Rapid weight loss

Scratching at his mouth or undue salivation could indicate a dental problem. If an ailment is suspected, have your puppy examined by the vet. If he is given a clean bill of health, try changing his food brand.

Keep it fresh

Puppy food, whether dry, semi-moist or wet, can 'go off', so follow the storage instructions and use-by date on the packaging. Large bags of food will go stale before you use it, unless you transfer it to an airtight container.

Clean living

With the joy of a puppy in your life comes the inevitable shed hair, slobbery licks, piles of faeces, puddles of urine and muddy paws. Maintaining hygiene rules to keep your home clean and tidy is vital for your puppy's and your family's comfort and well-being.

Puppy kisses

Dogs lick each other in greeting, while puppies tend to lick as a sign of submissiveness to older dogs and to the humans in their life. Puppies also lick humans to say hello. It's up to you whether you let your puppy lick you, but it's not very hygienic and can spread germs, especially if you allow him to lick your face.

Hair care

Daily grooming (see pages 162–163), especially for dense-coated breeds, will help to keep shed hair off flooring, furniture and soft furnishings. Vacuuming carpets, curtains and soft furnishings regularly, along with treating your puppy routinely against fleas (see pages 28–29), will help keep these pesky parasites under control. If you do suffer an infestation, your home will probably need fumigating to solve the problem.

Poop and puddles

Wearing rubber gloves, clean up your puppy's accidents around the home with kitchen roll and a poop scoop, then wash the area with a pet-stain cleaner that doesn't contain ammonia (a component of urine) so he isn't attracted to the same area to soil again.

Remove faeces from the garden daily and dispose of them safely, either in a dog toilet (available from pet stores) or with your household rubbish (check with your local authority). It's important to clear up mess to avoid it being trodden around the house and to prevent the spread of germs and parasites.

Worm your puppy regularly (see pages 28–29) and be vigilant in keeping your garden faeces-clear. It rarely occurs, but humans can catch toxocariasis from canines if they ingest *Toxocara canis* worm eggs.

Always wash your hands if your puppy licks you, after you've handled him and whenever you've cleaned up after him.

Wet feet

After a wet walk, avoid muddy pawprints on the floor, and the furniture receiving a shower from your puppy shaking himself dry, by wiping his feet and coat with an old towel on your return.

Grooming

Your puppy should enjoy being groomed as this is a great opportunity for the two of you to bond and spend time together. Some breeds need more attention than others, but all will benefit from a pampering session once or twice a week.

Essential equipment

Your puppy's breeder will advise on brushes and combs to buy so you can keep him looking his best. You can either groom your puppy on the floor or, depending on his size, on a sturdy table to make the job easier for you. It's a good idea to place a rubber mat on it for a firm footing. It's useful to have someone to help until he gets used to staying put. Never leave your pup by himself on a table in case he jumps or falls off it and hurts himself.

You can buy videos and books that demonstrate the best way to groom different breeds. Look out for these in pet stores and advertisements in dog magazines.

Beauty routine

How often you should groom your puppy depends on his coat type, but he'll love the attention no matter how often you want to brush him. As a general rule, follow the guidelines in the table opposite.

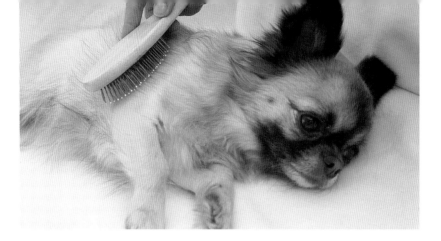

HOW OFTEN TO GROOM

Short coat	Groom weekly
Long and tangled coat	Groom daily to prevent double coats and matting
Curly and woolly coats	Groom every other day, professional trim every 4–8 weeks
Wire coat	Groom every day, professional hand-strip every 3–4 months

Important little places

When grooming, pay particular attention to behind your puppy's ears, inside the elbow crease, between his legs, under and along his tail, as these are all areas prone to matting. Clean his teeth too, using a brush and toothpaste made for dogs. Get your puppy's nails trimmed when they need it by a professional dog groomer or breeder.

Bathtime

Unless your puppy is a small, smooth, short-coated breed, the easiest way to bath him is to take him to a groomer with the facilities for washing and drying dogs. Puppies usually need bathing only when they get dirty or smelly – use tepid water, dog shampoo and conditioner. Bathing too much can strip the natural oils and make the skin and coat dry.

Wash your puppy's bed and bedding once a week to keep both sweet-smelling and to help control fleas. Also wash his toys, rinsing them well with clean water.

Out and about

Side by side

Getting out and about in town and country with your puppy is brilliant – and it's even better when he stays by your side on and off the lead when you tell him to. This gives you both security at times when he needs to stick to you like glue!

Stay with me

Teaching your puppy to stay by your side while out walking and come back to that position when called is vitally important. Sometimes there may be another dog off the lead, another person or a loose animal ahead, and you will want to keep your puppy under control next to you.

As explained on pages 68–69, the early stages of heel training comprise encouraging your puppy to stay next to you while on the lead, using food rewards as a lure. The next step is to teach him what the command 'Heel!' means.

Begin with your puppy on your left side and encourage him into position by your left leg by using a tasty treat. Say his name to gain his attention and, when you have it, walk forward saying 'Here!'. Hold another treat in your left hand so that he can see it and he will stay close to you in the hope of getting it. Avoid walking too fast for him to keep up.

When your puppy is in the required position, say 'Heel!' and after a couple of steps stop and reward him. This way, he learns the word by association with the position he's in when he gets the reward. If your pup lags behind or trots in front of you, don't say 'Heel!' to return him to the position at first as this will confuse him. Use treats instead. Only when he's learned where 'heel' is can you use the command to bring him back into position.

Once your puppy has learned to stay to heel on the lead, practise off-lead. Lots of rewards will pay dividends.

Watch out, puppy's about!

Remember always to stay alert when walking your puppy so that you are prepared for anything, such as him jumping up at people walking past or racing off after a cat he's spotted under a hedge. Other people – and especially the cat – may not appreciate his playful greeting!

Instant recall

You've already taught your puppy to come back to you when he's on his own in a safe enclosed space. You now need to take his education a step further to ensure he'll return to you when he's off-lead while out and about – immediately!

HOW TO TEACH YOUR DOG THE 'HERE!' COMMAND

1 Enlist the help of another person and have a pocketful of your puppy's favourite treats. Give him one and let him smell them in your pocket. Then ask the other person to play with him. Leave just a few metres between you to start with.

2 When they are having fun and your puppy is focused on that person, call him to you. Your helper should stop playing immediately, so that he loses interest and refocuses on you as being more rewarding. Bend down to welcome him with open arms and an encouraging voice. Call him again if necessary.

'Here!'

Before letting your puppy go off-lead so he can run free, for his safety you need to be certain that he will come back to you immediately on command. To be successful at this exercise, you need to make sure your puppy knows that you are more rewarding for him than whatever it is that has caught his attention, such as playing with a person or another dog.

3 As soon as he comes to you, give him lots of praise and some treats so that he learns that returning to you is pleasurable. Then let your puppy and helper resume the game, and repeat the exercise.

4 Practise over a period of time, with a person and another pup as well, to really instil the recall cue. Increase the distance between you a little at a time, decreasing it to go back a stage if necessary. Gradually reduce the reward to verbal praise alone, giving the occasional treat as an incentive.

Road sense

At first, your puppy won't be at all sure about road traffic. Cars, buses, lorries, motorbikes, cyclists, horse riders, trains – they are all loud, scary monsters to a young dog, until he learns that they are just part of the big, wide world he now inhabits.

Sound and vision

Your puppy needs to become accustomed to road traffic so he won't be frightened by it when you are walking him. Get him used to both day and night walking, so that he becomes comfortable with headlights as well as the noise, sight and smell of vehicles, in both dry weather and wet.

If he's small enough, carrying your puppy at first into the busy environment beyond the safe haven of your home and garden allows him to experience new situations from a safe vantage point.

Always keep your puppy on a lead when on or near a road, to prevent him running out and causing an accident or being knocked down.

Traffic shy

If your puppy has a real problem with traffic, find a quiet stretch of road where you can spend some time just sitting down and watching the world go by. Each time a vehicle approaches, distract your puppy by showing him a treat, then when the vehicle has passed let him have it. This way he learns to associate traffic and traffic noise with a rewarding experience.

In his shoes

The secret to successful traffic training – and, in fact, all new socialization encounters – is to try to look at things from your puppy's

point of view. Imagine what it is like being that small and vulnerable, with such limited knowledge. This being the case, avoid overwhelming him with too much traffic-spotting on one day: start with brief encounters and slowly build up until he is experiencing more and more. Make sure your puppy enjoys each encounter by giving him treats and talking happily and confidently to him. He will pick up on your lack of concern, learn that there is nothing to fear and become increasingly confident each time he meets traffic.

Top tip

Make a point of taking your puppy on buses and trains, even if you usually travel everywhere by car. If you ever do need to use public transport, it'll be less stressful for both of you.

Hitting the trail

Taking your puppy for walks – short ones at first – is a wonderful way to develop your relationship and improve his social skills. Your puppy will enjoy the experiences and adore spending quality time with you.

Spice of life

Variety is the key to keeping both you and your puppy content out walking. Try different routes regularly to keep things fresh and interesting. If you live near a dog-friendly park, nature reserve or beach, take him there in the car. Perhaps resolve to make one walk a week a special outing: you could involve the whole family, or other friends with their puppies, too.

Walking gear

Take toys and treats on walks to break up the routine, and also to implement short training sessions. Carry a basic human and canine first aid kit and your mobile phone in a light rucksack, along with toys, treats and poop bags to clean up after your puppy. Picking up faeces helps to keep walking areas clean and free from disease – and prevent dogs and their owners getting a bad name!

It's wise not to allow your puppy to do this in case the water is contaminated with chemicals or parasites. Take a collapsible drinking bowl and water in a bottle on longer walks, so you can be sure that when he takes a drink it's safe.

Your puppy might find things out on walks that he can't resist nibbling, such as dead birds and animals, and other animal dung. Don't shout at him, but steer him away by distracting him with play or a treat. Take food or carrion from him quickly in case it's laced with poison.

Remember: *never* allow your puppy to chase livestock. When walking through fields with animals, stay close to the edge so you can scramble out to get away from any over-curious creatures.

Good manners

For safety, put your puppy on the lead when you meet unfamiliar people and dogs (do the same when he's grown up). You may know your puppy is friendly, but other people don't and may be wary or even frightened if he charges up to them unannounced. Showing consideration to other dog walkers will be much appreciated.

Outdoor hazards

Some puppies love drinking from or splashing around in puddles or dirty ponds.

Dog trainers

Like toddlers, and then teenagers, puppies are into everything and can sometimes display a will of their own. Despite your best efforts, you may not be able to find a way to improve a particular type of behaviour. When this happens, you need to call in a puppy professor!

There are lots of dog trainers out there and you may have to check out quite a few before you are sure you have found the right one for you. Start by asking puppy-owning friends if they can recommend anyone, or consult your vet or the puppy's breeder. Alternatively, check local papers, the Internet and dog magazines.

Going to a trainer isn't admitting failure or defeat: it's doing the best thing you possibly can to make sure that you and your puppy develop that special and rewarding relationship you both deserve.

Making learning fun

Like choosing a school for a child, or a course for yourself, it's important to pick a dog trainer carefully. You need to find someone you like and can get on with, who shows a friendly and professional interest in you and your puppy, and who has the knowledge and experience to help you overcome problems by improving your handling skills.

Take a look

Once you have a shortlist, contact the trainers to explain your requirements and to see if they can help. If it seems positive, ask if you can go along to watch a training class, taking your puppy with you. A good trainer won't mind this – in fact, they might encourage it so they can get to know you and your puppy.

Training methods should be based on reward, be good-natured and positive, and the owners and their pets should be enjoying themselves. If you don't like what you see, try somewhere else.

Home help

If you are unable to travel to a trainer, try to find one who is prepared to come to you. Many trainers offer this service and it helps them to see exactly what the problem is *in situ*, so they can best advise how to solve it. This extra service may cost a bit more, but it can certainly be worth it.

Little lost puppy!

It'll probably never happen, but it's best to be prepared just in case your mischievous puppy goes missing. That way, you will stand the greatest chance of being reunited quickly with your precious pet. Knowing what action to take straight away can reap swift rewards.

Where's he gone?

There are a few reasons why a puppy might be there one minute and not the next.

- You thought he was safe in your puppy-proof garden, but someone left the gate open and your puppy decided to go off exploring.
- An opportunist thief spotted your puppy in the garden and has stolen him, or passing children have enticed him away to play with them.
- Your puppy has got stuck somewhere out of sight and sound range, perhaps in your shed or your neighbour's garage, and has fallen asleep.
- An adolescent unneutered puppy may have decided it's time to find a mate, so has gone to look for one.

Start looking

If you notice your puppy is missing, first check any nearby swimming pools and ponds. Next, check all the rooms in the house, in case he's come back in without you noticing and is contentedly asleep somewhere inside. Next, scour the garden and (with permission) those of your neighbours, asking them to let you know immediately if they see your puppy or bring him back to you. Then enlist friends and family to do a sweeping search of the area, starting close to home and gradually casting your net wider. If he's simply wandered, the chances are you'll find your puppy pretty quickly.

Please find my puppy!

If you haven't found your pup after an hour or so, alert your local dog warden, the police, and all the vet clinics and animal shelters in your area. It helps to provide them with a leaflet detailing your puppy's description, with a recent photograph printed on it if that is possible, and of course your contact details. You can also post these leaflets through neighbours' doors and ask permission to put them up in local stores. Perhaps place an advertisement in your local paper. Offering a reward for your puppy's safe return if found can often bring a swift and happy conclusion.

My puppy's
a genius!

Shake a paw

A puppy that greets visitors by shaking hands and then waves goodbye when they leave will certainly surprise your friends and family! This trick looks really impressive but is actually quite easy to teach, as holding out a paw is a dog's natural placatory gesture of submission.

HOW TO TEACH YOUR PUPPY THE 'SHAKE! AND WAVE!' COMMANDS

1 With your puppy in a sit (see pages 70–71), carefully take hold of his paw and lift it as you give the command 'Shake!', then shake it gently. Praise him and reward with a treat. Repeat four or five times. Next, stretch out a hand, palm upwards, and say 'Shake!'. As your puppy raises his paw, take it gently and shake it.

2 To teach your pup to wave, repeat the 'Shake!' command, but just as he stretches out his paw towards your hand lift your hand upwards just beyond his reach. Your puppy will then extend his leg to touch your hand. When he does so, give him lots of praise and a treat.

3 Next, delay the reward until he tries to touch your hand by giving a pawing movement. Vary your hand height, but not so high that it will stress him or force him to put down his paw for balance. When he is making a definite wave, change the command to 'Wave!'.

Find it!

Puppies just love to please their owners, so combine this with their natural instinct for seeking out 'prey' and you are on to a real winner! Getting your pet to find hidden objects provides great mutual entertainment, as well as an enjoyable training exercise for 'Find!' and 'Fetch!'.

Hide and seek

Hide and seek is a thrilling game for both puppies and children – so combine the two! First let the puppy see where the 'targets' hide and then encourage him to 'Find!' them. Both you and the children must praise him hugely when he does. Then see if he can succeed when you don't let him see where they have hidden. The children may need to call him until he learns to scent them out.

Treasure hunt

Hiding treats in the house and garden is another fun way of teaching your puppy to 'Find!'. Let him sniff them and taste one, then allow him to see where you put them and tell him to 'Find!' – when he does, his reward is the treat and your praise. Once your puppy has got the idea, taste and scent, hide the treats without letting him see where you put them and tell him to 'Find!'.

HOW TO TEACH YOUR PUPPY THE 'FIND!' COMMAND

1 Encourage your puppy to sniff a favourite toy or a treat, then let him watch as you partially conceal it under an old blanket, newspaper or box.

2 Position yourselves a metre or so away from the target where he can see and smell it. He'll be focused on the object and keen to go and get it, so point to it and say 'Find!' or 'Seek!', then let him go, encouraging him to 'Find!' and repeating the command if needed until he finds it.

3 Once your puppy has retrieved the object, praise him enthusiastically and encourage him to bring it back to you to play, saying 'Fetch!' (see pages 82–83).

4 When your pup understands, conceal the object completely, move further away and encourage him to find it, so that he learns to develop his scenting skill.

My puppy's a genius! **183**

Hooping it up

Although you can't do fancy tricks involving jumping while your puppy's precious body is still growing and strengthening, you can still have plenty of fun preparing the groundwork to make your pal a top circus star. All you need is a hoop!

A great game

Initially, leave the hoop where your puppy can see, smell and get used to it. This is so that he views it as nothing to be scared of. If he's a bit unsure, occasionally leave a treat next to it, so he associates the hoop with something rewarding when greed overcomes his fear.

After a day or two, when your puppy is perfectly content with the hoop being part of the furniture, carry it around while you are with him. Again, give him rewards while you are holding the hoop to reinforce a positive association with it. Then you can begin teaching him the hoop trick.

HOW TO TEACH YOUR PUPPY THE 'HOOP!' COMMAND

1 Hold the hoop steady on the ground and have your puppy sitting on one side of it. Then use a delicious, smelly treat to lure him through it, saying 'Here!' at the same time (see pages 44–45).

2 Praise him when he goes through the hoop and give him his reward once he's on the other side. Be sure to keep the hoop still and resting on the ground, or have someone hold it secure for you – if it moves, it may frighten him and he may be reluctant to try again.

3 Repeat several times, gradually substituting the treats with verbal praise only. Add 'Hoop!' to your command of 'Here!'. Once your puppy's got the hang of it, have him sit and stay at one side of the hoop (see pages 70–75) until you give him the command 'Here, hoop!'. In the end, you can drop the 'Here!'.

'Speak!'

Finally, wouldn't it be great if dogs could speak? Well, they can! Not literally, of course, but it is possible to train your puppy to bark on command, which can come in useful. At the very least, people will be amazed by your 'talking' puppy.

Good to talk

In this trick, your puppy is told to 'speak' on cue by barking. Some breeds bark more than others, so are easier to train to do this trick. Particularly good barking breeds are Terriers (such as Jack Russells), working dogs (such as the Newfoundland), utility dogs (such as Poodles) and terrier-type mongrels.

Top tip

Your puppy needs to know when to start and when to stop barking. It's important that barking is not rewarded when he does it without you having given the order.

Teach the command 'Quiet!' as a cue to stop, or refrain from, barking. To do this, start rewarding him with a treat whenever he stops barking, saying 'Quiet!' as you do. Gradually dispense with treats, using only praise to reward. You can even replace the vocal command with a visual cue (one that can't be confused with other visual cues) to tell the puppy to be quiet.

HOW TO TEACH YOUR PUPPY THE 'SPEAK!' COMMAND

1 Put your puppy in the sit position (see pages 70–75). Stand with his favourite toy or a treat above his head. Tempt him with the object, moving it and talking excitedly, then use the command 'Speak!'.

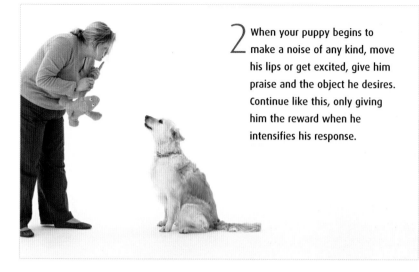

2 When your puppy begins to make a noise of any kind, move his lips or get excited, give him praise and the object he desires. Continue like this, only giving him the reward when he intensifies his response.

3 Build progressively on each 'Speak' command, until your puppy makes a noise immediately on receiving the verbal command. Then add a visual cue, such as a finger to your lips or a nod of your head, so that eventually you can dispense with the verbal command entirely.

Index

a

ACER principles 70
adenoviral hepatitis,
      vaccination for 30
aggression 48, 65, 109, 111,
      114, 117, 118, 119, 126,
      129
allergy 159
anaemia 28
animal shelters 15
animals, other 46–47, 61,
      173
ankle-biting 62
anthropomorphism 25
anti-testosterone drug 127
anxiety 119

b

Barker's Birthday Cake 27
barking training 150–151,
      186
bathing 163
bed 17, 24, 35
bedding 17
bedtime 38–39
begging for food 67,
      156–157
behaviour 52–53, 56–57,
      60–61
   at mealtimes 66–67
birds, caged 46
birth control 127
blanket barking 150
boarding kennels 30,
      102–103, 137

body language 84, 106,
      107, 108–109, 111, 116,
      130–131
bones, chewing 18–19
Border Collie 10, 55
Border Terrier 11
Bordetella bronchiseptica,
      vaccination for 30
boredom 119, 138–139,
      152
breeds 12–13

c

cancer 128
canine hairdressing 11;
      see also grooming
canine parainfluenza,
      vaccination for 30
canine parvovirus,
      vaccination for 30
car travel 17, 94–95
carrion 173
castration *see* neutering
cats 46, 166
Cavalier King Charles Spaniel
      8
chasing 61, 166, 173
chewing 41, 124,
      152–153
Chihuahua 8
children 36, 48, 50–51,
      115
chocolate 25
clicker training 88–89, 115
cocked head 130

Cockerpoo 9
collar 17, 24, 69
collar and lead training
      60
commands: Down 76–77
   Eat 73
   Fetch 82–83, 183
   Find 182, 183
   Finish 53, 55
   Give 83
   Go to bed 80–81, 140
   Heel 68, 166
   Here 45, 53, 75, 145, 166,
      184, 185
   Hoop 185
   Leave 72–73
   No 55, 65, 148
   Open wide 48
   Quiet 186
   Roll over 78–79
   Shake 180–181
   Shut the door 140
   Sit 53, 70–71, 76, 147
   Speak 186–187
   Stand 76
   Stay 53, 67, 73, 74–75,
      76, 81, 140
   Watch 115
   Wave 181
communication 84,
      106–111
contentment 112–113
crate 40–41, 94–95
   training 60 *see also* den;
      travel crate

cross-bred puppies 8–9
cues *see* hand signals 84

d
Dalmatian 117
DAP (dog-appeasing pheromone) diffuser 118, 119
dehydration 121
den 35, 36, 122; *see also* crate
dental problems 159
digestive upset 121
distemper virus, vaccination for 30
distraction techniques 65, 92, 113, 173
docked tails 111
Dobermann 8, 117
dog breeders 14, 15
dog coat 17
dog grille/guard 17, 95
dog sitters 137
dog-speak 84, 106–107
dog trainers 174–175
dog walkers 137
dog-walking groups 97
door courtesy 142–143
doors, shutting 140–141
doorways 140
Down command 76–77
drink 18

e
Eat command 73
emotions 25, 108
environment 119
equipment 16–17

exercise 10, 124–125; *see also* walks
eye contact 114–115

f
facial expressions 116–117
faeces, disposal of 17, 161, 172
fear 65, 109, 111
posture 130–131
Fetch command 82–83, 183
Find command 182, 183
Find it 87, 182–183
Finish command 53, 55
flea treatments 29
fleas 28, 160
floors, slippery 37
Follow the leader 87
food/feeding 18–19, 24–25, 159
begging 67, 156–157
stealing 67
food bowl 17
food chews 153
food refusal 158–159
food training 60, 66–67
food treats 18–19, 36, 45, 66, 80
recipes 26–27
furniture etiquette 148–149

g
games 86–87
garden safety 22–23
German Shepherd 55, 130–131
getting lost 176–177
Give command 83

Go to bed command 80–81, 140
Golden Retriever 11
grabbing 97, 113
Great Dane 18
Greyhound 10, 79
grooming 11, 139, 160, 162–163
kit 17
gums 19, 48
gut damage 28

h
hair, shed 160
hamsters 46
hand signals 71, 74, 84–85, 187
handling 48–49
hearing, testing 121
Heel command 68, 166
Here command 45, 53, 75, 145, 166, 184, 185
Hide and seek 87, 182
Hoop trick 184–185
house rules 52–53
hygiene 19, 160–161, 163
hyperactivity 124

i
identity disc 17
illness, signs of 120
indoor kennel 17
insurance 100
Irish Water Spaniel 10

j
Jack Russell 186
jumping up 146–147, 154

k

kennel cough 30
Kennel Kiss Cookies 26
Kong toys 83, 134, 137, 153

l

Labradoodle 9
large breeds 12, 13
lead 17
    walking on 68–69
learning 53–54, 56, 125
Leave command 72–73
leaving puppy alone
    136–137
leptospirosis, vaccination for
    30, 31
licking 146, 160
lifestyle 10–13
livestock 61, 173

m

malnutrition 28
mealtime behaviour 66–67
medium-sized breeds 13
Mexican Hairless dog 11
mongrels 9, 186

n

nails, trimming 163
name training 44
naming 44–45
nanny dogs 99
nervousness 121
neutering 119, 127,
    128–129
Newfoundland 186
No command 55, 65, 148
noises 92–93, 119

o

obsessive behaviour 107,
    124
Open wide command 48
overfeeding 66

p

pack hierarchy 47
pampering 24–25
parasites 28, 160
patience training 60, 62–63
paw raising 130
people, puppies and 93,
    96–97, 146–147; see
    also visitors
pesticides 23
pests see parasites
pet carrier 34–35, 95
pet stores 15
pets, other 46–47
pheromones 127
play 54–55, 86–87, 124–125
play-biting 55, 56–57
poisoning 23, 173
Poodle 11, 186
poop scoop 17, 160
praise 45, 64, 69, 71, 73, 76
problem behaviour 154
puberty see sexual maturity
public transport 171
pulse 121
puppy: acquiring 14–15
    age on leaving mother 14
    bringing home 34–35
    and children 36, 48,
      50–51, 115
    choosing 8–13
    contented 112–113

equipment 16–17
feeding 18–19, 24–25, 159
grooming 11, 139, 160,
    162–163
handling 48–49
health 28–31, 120–121
leaving alone 136–137
lost 176–177
naming 44–45
and other pets 46–47
pampering 24–25
and people 93, 96–97,
    146–147, 173
price 15
settling in 36–39
and traffic 93, 170–171
training plan 60–61
unhappy 118–119
at the vet 100–101
vital signs 121
and visitors 134,
    142–143
puppy area 20, 36
puppy farms 15
puppy parties 99, 101
puppy shower 16
puppy training classes
    98–99
pure-bred puppies 8

q

Quiet command 186

r

rabbits, pet 46
rabies, vaccination for 30
recall 45, 168–169
respect 113

respiration 121
rewards 44, 45, 46, 52, 63, 64, 66, 69, 88
Roll over command 78–79
rolling 131
roundworms 28

S
safety: in garden 22–23
  in house 20, 37
  on walks 173
Saluki 9
sandpit 139
scent-marking 126
scraps 157, 158, 159
season, coming into 126–127
Setter 55
sexual maturity 119, 126–129
Shake a paw 180–181
Shake command 180–181
Shih Tzu 11
showing 30
Shut the door command 140
shyness 121
Sit command 53, 70–71, 76
sit-stay 75
sleep 37, 38–39
small breeds 12, 13
'smilers' 117
social skills/socializing 56, 96–97, 110
socialization training 60, 61, 92–93, 98–99, 122
spaying see neutering
Speak command 186–187

sporting dogs 10
stair gate 37, 53, 157
Stand command 76
Stay command 53, 67, 73, 74–75, 76, 81, 140
stereotypies see obsessive behaviour
strays 15
stress 37, 62, 101, 107
stroking 48

t
tail positions 111
tail wagging 107, 110–111
tapeworms 28
teeth 19, 48, 163
temperature 121
Terriers 55, 117, 138, 186
time out 61, 62, 65
toilet training 35, 36, 40, 42–43, 60
  accidents 20, 42, 95, 160
toxocariasis 161
toys 17, 36, 37, 87, 138, 157
  activity 40, 152
  chew 37, 56, 153
  for fetching 83
  Kong 83, 134, 137, 153
traffic 93, 170–171
training classes 174–175
training plan 60–61
travel, car 17, 94–95
travel crate 34–35, 94–95
travel harness 95
travel sickness 35, 95
travel training 61, 94–95, 171

Treasure hunt 87, 182
treats, food 18–19, 36, 45, 66, 80
  recipes 26–27
tricks: Hoop 184–185
  Shake a paw 180–181
  'Speak!' 186–187

U
unhappiness 118–119
utility dogs 186

V
vaccination 30–31
vet/vet clinic 99, 100–101
visitors 134, 142–143
vital signs 121

W
Wait command see Stay
walks 125, 139, 166, 172–173
  teaching to wait 144–145
Watch command 115
water bowl 17
water safety 23
Wave command 181
Whippet 79
working dogs 138, 186
worming 28–29, 161

Acknowledgements

Picture acknowledgements:
Getty Images 102; Frank Herholdt 164; Ryuichi Sato 103.

Octopus Publishing Group Limited/Angus Murray 9, 11, 42, 49,
60, 62, 67, 68, 74, 80, 81, 81, 110, 116, 127, 142; /Rosie Hyde 47,
130, 131; /Russell Sadur 2, 6, 8, 14, 15, 16, 17, 19, 20, 22,
23, 24, 25, 26, 27, 28, 29, 31, 32, 34, 35, 37, 38, 40, 43, 46, 51,
53, 54, 55, 57, 58, 64, 65, 70, 71, 72, 76, 84, 85, 86, 88, 90, 92,
93, 94, 95, 96, 98, 99, 100, 101, 104, 107, 111, 112, 115, 117,
118, 120, 123, 124, 125, 125, 127, 128, 132, 135, 136, 136, 138,
139, 140, 141, 144, 144, 145, 147, 148, 149, 149, 151, 152, 153,
153, 156, 157, 158, 159, 160, 162, 163, 166, 170, 171, 172, 173,
173, 175, 176, 177, 178, 180, 186; /Steve Gorton 18, 36, 39, 44,
45, 52, 62, 66, 78, 82, 83, 87, 97, 101, 106, 108, 109, 114, 118,
119, 121, 122, 136, 146, 150, 161, 168, 174, 175, 182, 184.

Executive Editor Trevor Davies
Editor Amy Corbett
Executive Art Editor Leigh Jones
Designer Nicola Liddiard
Production Manager David Hearn
Picture Library Assistant Ciaran O'Reilly